Vintage Jewelry

A Price and Identification Guide ◆ 1920-1940s

Leigh Leshner

Published by

**krause
publications**

700 East State Street • Iola, WI 54990-0001
715/445-2214 • FAX: 715/445-4087   www.krause.com

Please call or write for our free catalog of publications. Our
toll-free number to place an order or obtain a free catalog is
(800) 258-0929.

Library of Congress Catalog Number: 2002105081
ISBN: 0-87349-423-7

Photography by Maurice Childs.

Jewelry provided from the personal collections of author
Leigh Leshner, Carol Leshner, and Marcia Brown.

Table of Contents

Acknowledgments   4

Introduction   5

White Metal and Rhinestone Jewelry, 1920s-1940s   6

The History of Rhinestones   10

Cuts and Shapes of Rhinestones   12

Settings   14

Metals   16

Collecting Jewelry   18

Price and Identification Guide   20

About the Author   206

Bibliography   207

Index   208

Acknowledgments

I wish to thank my parents, Robert and Carol Leshner, for their never-ending encouragement and support in all that I do.

Thanks also to:

Vintage Fashion and Costume Jewelry editor Lucille Tempesta and author Marcia Brown for their editorial expertise.

Matthew Ribarich for providing stones from his almost five million-stone inventory of costume and antique jewelry replacement stones.

Maurice Childs for the photography.

Carol Leshner and Marcia Brown for providing jewelry from their private collections.

All those at Krause Publications who helped make this book a reality: my editor Maria Turner, page designer Jamie Martin, and acquisitions editor Paul Kennedy.

Introduction

At a very young age, I fell in love with antique and vintage jewelry.

The 1920s through the 1940s gave us wonderful pieces of jewelry made of all types of white metal and rhinestones. It is a world within itself, full of history, beauty, and mystery.

Costume jewelry is reflective of the times as well as the social and aesthetic movements. Each piece tells its own story through hidden clues that, when interpreted, help solve the mysteries surrounding them.

The jewelry is at times rich and elegant, and at other times, ornate yet simple. The pieces range in size and vary from delicate to bold. Whether you are looking for elaborate pieces or simple beauty, you are able to find it in the jewelry made during this time period.

The number of collectors has grown dramatically. With the advent of the computer and the Internet, it has become viable for people to shop at home to connect with other dealers and collectors and add to their growing collections.

Increased interest has led collectors, dealers, and people who have inherited old jewelry to ask a lot of questions. They now want to know what it is made of, what the history behind the piece is, how old it is, and the most common question—what is it worth?

By providing examples and historical information, this book will answer these often-asked questions.

White Metal and Rhinestone Jewelry, 1920s-1940s

Costume jewelry was an outgrowth of the desire of the average person to have copies of the real jewelry that had previously been reserved for the wealthy.

Costume jewelry began its steady ascent to popularity in the 1920s. Since it was relatively inexpensive to produce, there was mass production. The sizes and designs of the jewelry varied. Often, it was worn a few times, disposed of, and then replaced with a new piece. It was thought of as expendable—a cheap throwaway to dress up an outfit.

Costume jewelry became so popular that it was sold in both the upscale fine stores and the five-and-dimes.

Even though the cost was relatively low, each piece brought pleasure to its wearer. The designs had an intrinsic beauty that made each piece unique and special. Designs ranged from the subtle to the outrageous.

Because of the relatively inexpensive production costs, designers were able to unleash their creativity, while at the same time maintain high production standards. Many of the designers had a background in fine jewelry-making, and they brought their knowledge and skill to this rather new phenomena of "fake" jewelry. These were jewelers who were used to working with gemstones. They now were able to take their glorious designs and interpret them into costume jewelry for the average woman. The quality was unsurpassed, and the designs were unique and often rivaled their "real" counterparts.

Many pieces were made by well-recognized designers and companies, but a greater percentage of the jewelry was unsigned. But both the signed and unsigned pieces were works of art. The designers were free to express themselves in an unbridled fashion that was evident in the designs that ranged from whimsical to elegant.

Just as with any other item, there was a wide range of quality in terms of the materials used. Pieces ranged from low-end base metal to higher-end sterling. Although the materials may have been different in terms of perceived quality, the finished product was a sight to behold. The designs included flowers, figures, bows, Art Deco designs, animals, geometric patterns, and much more. The designers not only used rhinestones to enhance the metal, but they also incorporated molded glass, beads, faux pearls, and semiprecious stones. Enameling techniques were often used to add color.

Coco Chanel was well-regarded as a designer of couture fashions that embodied creativity and individuality. Her designs were trend-setting, and it was Chanel who helped make costume jewelry acceptable. Subscribing to the notion that imitation is the sincerest form of flattery, she often wore her real jewelry alongside her costume creations. This enhanced her couture wear and added that touch of glamour that women were looking for.

The 1920s was an overlap of styles consisting of Edwardian, Art Nouveau, and Art Deco. Many of the pieces incorporated the graceful and naturalistic curving of the Art Nouveau styles, while others had an Edwardian look that imitated the platinum and diamonds that were prevalent of this style. These designs were imitations made to look like their real counterparts.

But the predominant style of the times was Art Deco. The designs were geometric and bold. They were streamlined, stylized, and angular. The Art Deco movement got its beginning in Paris at the Exposition Internationale des Arts Decoratifs et Industriales Modernes.

For the most part, the 1920s were known as the "White Period." This referred to the prevalent use of clear rhinestones set in white metal. Gradually, the jewelry moved toward bolder colors. White metal was accented with dramatic colored stones in ruby, sapphire, emerald, black, amethyst, and topaz.

The clothing of the times influenced jewelry designs. Women had now begun moving toward shorter, slim, drop-waisted dresses. The hemlines were rising, and stockings were in vogue. The materials being used for the clothing were lighter and more sheer. This clothing trend led to women wearing delicate chokers and pendants as well as long dangling earrings and multiple bracelets. Furs and boas were also popular. Fur clips and bold brooches were worn to adorn them.

The 1930s was considerably quieter than the '20s. With the Depression and the advent of World War II, times were changing, including changes in jewelry designs. The lines were softened. Jewelry was a bit simpler than in the 1920s, though not too simplistic.

Jewelry now provided a respite. Women could purchase a relatively inexpensive piece of jewelry to spruce up an old outfit to make it look new. Designers made wonderful whimsical designs of birds, flowers, circus animals, bows, dogs, and just about every other figural imaginable. Through the use of enameling and colored rhinestones, the jewelry was bright and festive.

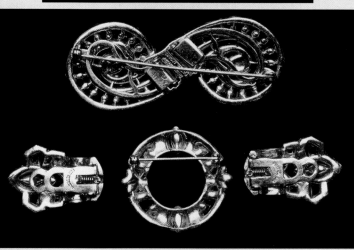

Duettes, fronts and backs.

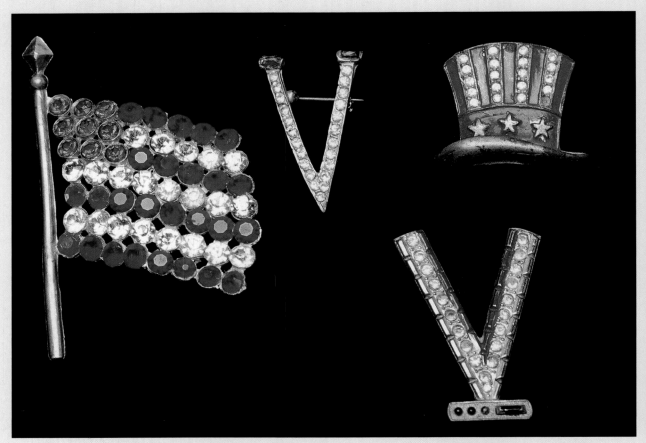

Many pieces made from 1920 and into the '40s carried a patriotic theme. Both those who made the pieces as well as those who wore them saw these jewelry designs as a way to support the war effort.

Jewelry of the '30s was also functional. In 1931, Coro patented the "Duette," and in 1936, Trifari patented the "Clipmate." Both of these creations were brooches that consisted of two dress clips or fur clips that would come apart from the pin and could be worn separately or as one large brooch.

The 1940s took the designs to bigger and bolder heights. The jewelry had a more substantial feel to it and many designers began using larger stones to enhance the dramatic pieces. Common themes running throughout the designs were bows, flowers, and sunbursts.

Reflecting the mood of the country, the clothing had a very militaristic feel to it. The predominant materials used were rayon, wool, and linen. The clothing had big boxy shoulders and slim skirts accented by stockings and high heels. Again, fur was very much in style and large bold fur clips often adorned it.

Patriotism was also running high, and sweetheart jewelry became fashionable. This

Trembler brooch, back and front.

jewelry was made and worn as a sign of the support for the war effort and as sentimental treasures for those that were fighting the war. Common themes of this jewelry were American flags, a V-sign for victory, Uncle Sam's hat, airplanes, anchors, and eagles.

The designers' creations using white metal and rhinestones were unlimited. They began using spring mechanisms to create jewelry that moved, called tremblers. Parts of the jewelry, such as the stamen of a flower, would be attached to a small, coiled piece of wire that allowed it to move as the wearer moved.

The beautiful designs were incorporated into rings, bracelets, necklaces, brooches, earrings, dress clips, shoe clips, fur clips, Duettes, scarf holders, stickpins, double pins, belt buckles, hat pins, bangles, and hair ornaments. Designers' imaginations were left unbound and unrestricted by the outlets available for them to incorporate their masterpieces.

Clothing became the background to showcase these wonderful pieces. Women began wearing clips and pins on hats. Belts were adorned with rhinestone buckles and brooches. Dress clips were worn in the V of a neckline or in the square of a neckline.

Dress clips were prevalent during this period, so they are readily available and easily found. However, they are often overlooked because people don't know how to wear them.

Dress clips can be worn in many ways. They can be worn in the traditional manner—in the V or square of a neckline.

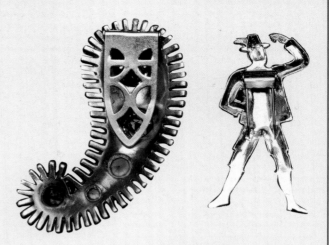

Dress clip (left) and fur clip.

They can be slipped over a cord or chain and worn as a necklace. They also can be clipped onto a pocket or placed on a rolled-up sleeve. Hats can be adorned with them. They can be converted into a brooch by placing a safety pin inside a shirt or jacket so that the pin bar goes through the material, and then the clip is dropped over the pin bar.

With clothing the backdrop to showcase many jewelry pieces, brooches, like the ones shown here, became very much a part of every fashionable woman's wardrobe.

The History of Rhinestones

Czechoslovakian glass, or Bohemian glass as it was originally known, had its beginnings in the thirteenth and fourteenth centuries in Bohemia, a part of the Czech Republic. The country has a history rich in glassmaking, including hand-blown, molded, and cut glass. The introduction of lead compounds is responsible for the clarity and brilliance of the glass and is known as lead crystal.

The center of Czechoslovakian jewelry production was Gablonz, where there had always been a tradition of glassmaking.

Glass was not limited to functional objects. By 1918, the Czechoslovakian glass industry began to use innovative and creative techniques and incorporated them in jewelry designs. Thousands of people worked out of their homes as glass pressers, grinders, and cutters to make perfume bottles, vanity items, beads, and rhinestones.

The rhinestones were manmade gemstones from highly refined glass. The glass was first colored the desired color by the introduction of various metals and then pressed into molds to create the final shape. Each stone was ground and polished on all facets by machine to extract the brilliance. The stones were generally foiled. This opaque back coating increases the reflectivity and brilliance while allowing the back of the stone to be glued into the setting without seeing the glue.

Rhinestones are often referred to as paste. Originally, paste was glass that was ground into a paste, molded, and then melted. The final piece was an opaque, dense glass with a frosted surface. The paste would have numerous air bubbles and swirl marks, but the highly leaded glass was cut with facets to reflect the light, and it was backed by a copper or silver lining. When the term paste is currently used, it generally refers to rhinestones. While the United States refers to the term rhinestone, the terms paste, strass, and diamente are often used in Europe.

The term rhinestone came from the Rhine River in Austria. In the late-1800s, the river was filled with quartz pebbles in brilliant colors. As this source was depleted, imitation glass rhinestones replaced them. Rhinestones are highly reflective glass made to imitate gems. They are molded, leaded glass of all colors. A rhinestone is always backed with a thin metallic layer of gold or silver to bounce the light off the glass for brilliancy and to create a sparkling quality.

In 1891, Daniel Swarovski revolutionized the jewelry business when he created a new glass-cutting machine that could mechanically cut faceted glass. Previously, it would take long periods of time to finish the stones by hand. Now, the stones could be created in a fraction of the time. Swarovski had a background in glassmaking, and he soon began making rhinestones with a 32 percent high lead content that produced faceted stones with refractions unrivaled by any other companies.

Swarovski also revolutionized the rhinestone business by creating vacuum plating for the backs of the stones with silver and gold. By doing this, he again reduced the need for hand labor. After all of his efforts, ingenuity, and imagination, Swarovski's stones today, thought of as the highest quality rhinestones, are used by more than 85 percent of the American jewelry companies.

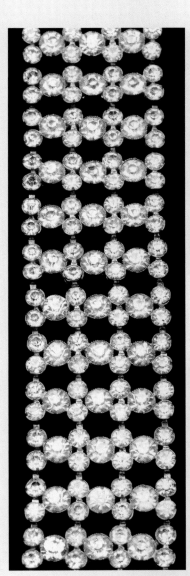

Czechoslovakia has a rich history in glassmaking, and by extension, jewelry-making. Shown above is a Czechoslovakian bracelet with clear rhinestones.

Daniel Swarovski revolutionized the rhinestone business by creating vacuum plating for the backs of stones with silver and gold. Although contemporary jewelry often carries the Swarovski name, vintage pieces did not. Yet, much of the older rhinestone jewelry was indeed made with brilliant Swarovski rhinestones, like the pieces shown above and below.

Cuts and Shapes of Rhinestones

Rhinestones are both affordable and fashionable. They come in many shapes and sizes. The various cuts are:

Baguette: A narrow, elongated rectangular-shaped faceted stone.

Cabochon: A round dome-shaped stone with a flat back, usually opaque or translucent.

Chaton: A stone that has eight facets on top and eight facets on the bottom. The top is flat, and the bottom comes to a point. There are several parts of a chaton. The flat top is known as a table. The girdle is the place where the top and the bottom of the stone meet. The crown is the part of the stone that is above the girdle. The pavilion is the bottom part of the stone under the girdle. The culet is the point of the stone.

Cushion cut: Rhinestones are not cut in this fashion. It is a term used for gemstones only.

Dentelle: A stone that is formed in a mold and then hand-cut. There are 18, 32, or 64 facets on the back and front of the stone, and light is refracted through the facets in the surface of the stone.

Emerald cut: A square-cut stone with faceted edges.

Flat-back rhinestone: The top of the stone is faceted, and the back is flat.

Marquis, oval, or navette: The stone is oval-shaped, there is a point on each side of the stone, and it has a flat top.

Mine cut: A square stone with rounded corners, sometimes called a cushion shape. Thirty-two crown facets and 24 pavilion facets with a table and a culet.

Pear cut: A teardrop-shaped stone.

Princess cut: A square-cut stone, sometimes now known as a quadrillium or squarillion cut.

Rose cut: A flat-base stone with 24 triangular facets meeting at the top with a point.

Round cut: See flat-back rhinestone.

Square octagon cut: See emerald cut.

Tapered baguette: A narrow, elongated rectangular-shaped faceted stone that is largest at one end and then slims down toward the other end.

Triangle cut: A triangular-cut faceted stone based on a brilliant style cut.

Please note: A mine cut, princess cut, and rose cut are types of cuts that are generally used for real gemstones, though some have occasionally been used for semiprecious stones such as garnets and on very rare occasions for rhinestones. I've included them above because the terms are often bandied about, but collectors should be aware that these cuts are rarely used for rhinestones.

Did you know?

Often molded glass is incorporated into the designs. One commonly used type of molded glass is known as fruit salad. While the glass looks like it is carved, it is actually molded to give the illusion of carving.

Settings

Several different types of settings are used for the rhinestones.

Bead set: Small burrs of metal rise out of the base of the pin to hold the individual rhinestones in place.

Hand set: Stones are glued in individually in the scooped-out cup in the metal.

Bezel set: A way of setting the stone in which the stone is held in place by a band of metal that is placed around the outside of each stone. This is a time-consuming and expensive method.

Hand set with metal prongs: Stones are handset and then the metal prongs are bent over the top of the stone.

Channel set: Occurs when the rhinestones rest in a metal channel and are held in only by a slight rim that runs along the edge of the channel. In this method, the stones are set side by side so no metal is seen between the stones.

Pave set: Occurs when the stones are set together in a group so that the underlying metal surface is hidden.

Example of a bead setting.

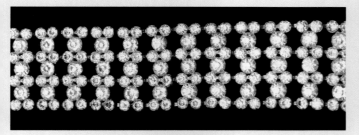

Example of a bezel setting.

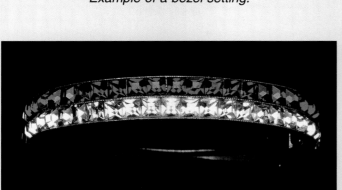

Example of a channel setting.

Example of a hand setting.

Example of a hand set with metal prongs.

Example of a pave setting.

Metals

There were many types of white metals used in the 1920s, '30s, and '40s in the production of jewelry.

Base metal: Nonprecious metals that include zinc, tin, and lead.

Chromium: A hard gray white metal often used in Art Deco jewelry.

Nickel silver: A white metal mixture of copper, zinc, and nickel.

Pewter: A leaded alloy.

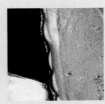

Pot metal: A mixture of metals that were all thrown into a pot and melted down. It was prevalent and is recognizable due to its dull-looking finish.

Rhodium: A non-tarnishing white metal that resembles platinum. It has a shiny, bright veneer. It is an expensive finish and is often used to plate base metals to give them a platinum-like sheen.

Sterling: A silver compound that contains 92.5 percent silver. Sterling silver will usually be hallmarked with the word "sterling" or an assay mark on the back of the piece of jewelry. This metal type was widely used during World War II because the other metals traditionally used in jewelry production were being used for the war effort.

White metal: A mixture of 92 percent tin with cadmium, lead, and zinc.

Did you know?

Base metal, nickel silver, and white metal all look very similar to pot metal.

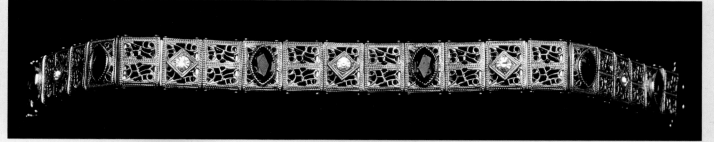

Chromium

Pot metal

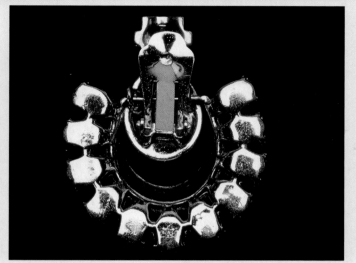

Rhodium

Sterling

Collecting Jewelry

There are many factors that determine value and collectibility. Among these factors are current fashion trends, demand and rarity, quality of craftsmanship and design, and the condition of the piece.

Over the years, there has been a misconception that only signed pieces have value. This simply is not true. Although some of the better-known and more collectible designers who designed during this period, including Eisenberg, Trifari, Coro, Corocraft, Reja, De Rosa, McClelland Barclay, Marcel Boucher, Hattie Carnigie, Ciner, Hobe, Mazer, Pennino, Nettie Rosenstein, Elsa Schiaparelli, and Weiss, created beautiful jewelry, some of the best examples of costume jewelry are unsigned.

As a collector, you should buy what you like and don't necessarily worry about trends. In fact, if what you like isn't in vogue at the moment, consider yourself lucky! Chances are you'll be able to add more pieces to your collection for less money.

Price alone shouldn't dictate your choices either. A purchase made for only a few dollars may not enhance your collection, but you don't have to be a millionaire to own wonderful old pieces. You can still find wonderful sleepers out there at garage sales, flea markets, estate sales, antique shows, rummage sales, and on the Internet.

Focus on condition and quality as the underlying rule for collecting. After that, let your imagination and desires run wild! A collection can consist of a specific type of jewelry such as bracelets. Or you may choose to focus on a particular design style such as Art Deco. Or a collection of bird pins may be just the collection for you.

Whatever you choose to collect, have fun with it and enjoy the beauty and history behind each piece in your collection.

Several unsigned pieces above.

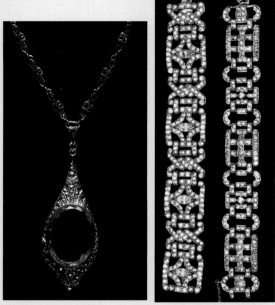

Three Art Deco pieces above, all unsigned.

When collecting vintage rhinestone jewelry, remember it does not have to be signed to be beautiful— and valuable. Compare the unsigned pieces at the top of the page with the Pennino pieces at right.

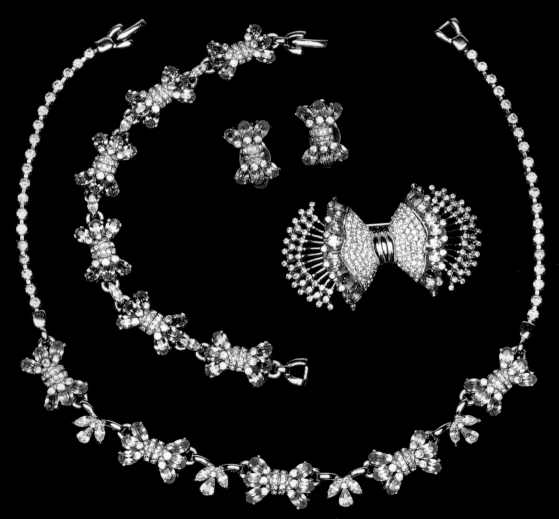

Pennino necklace, earrings, bracelet, and brooch.

Price and Identification Guide

F ollowing is a price and identification guide
featuring thousands of fine examples of vintage
jewelry from the 1920s through the 1940s. There are
both signed and unsigned pieces contained within the price
guide, but the majority are unsigned, as the goal of this book
is to show not only the beauty—but also the value—of
unsigned vintage white metal and rhinestone jewelry.

Please remember that values in this price guide are listed
only to help determine a reference point. Values vary
according to each piece's condition, quality, design, and/or
geographic location where the piece is purchased.

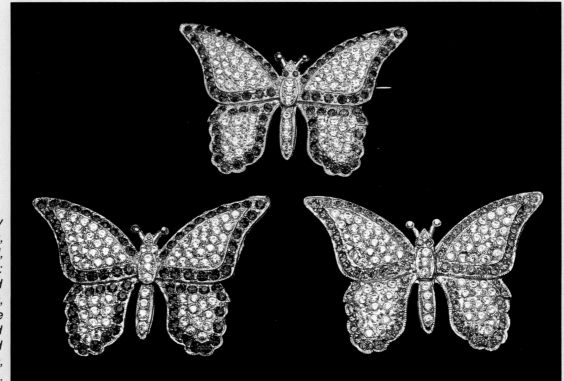

Identical butterfly brooches, all pot metal, clockwise from top: with clear and amethyst rhinestones, with clear and blue rhinestones, and with clear and green rhinestones, $110 each.

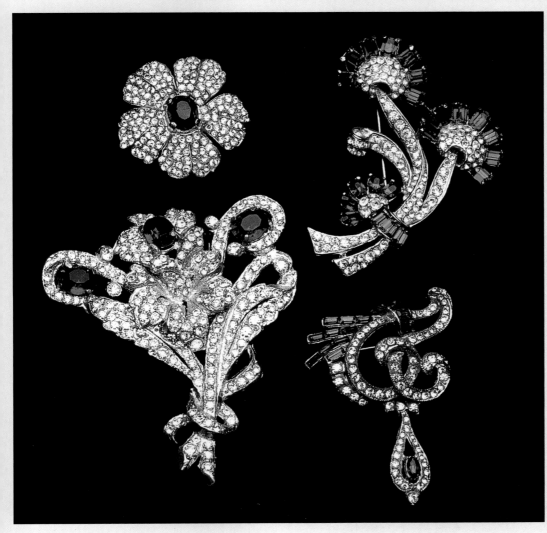

Clear and green rhinestone pieces, clockwise from top left: Trifari rhodium fur clip, $165; rhodium flower brooch, $125; pot metal brooch, $135; and pot metal floral bouquet brooch, $145.

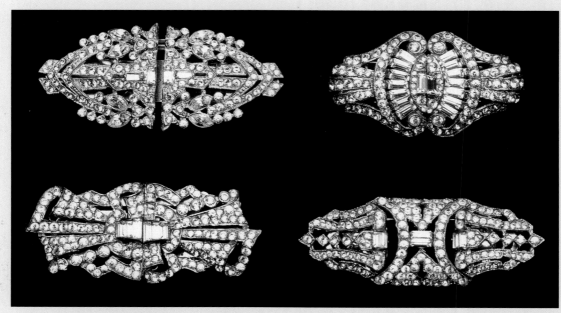

Assorted pieces with clear rhinestones, clockwise from top left: pot metal Clipmate, $110; Coro Duette, $195; pot metal Clipmate, $125; and pot metal Duette, $125.

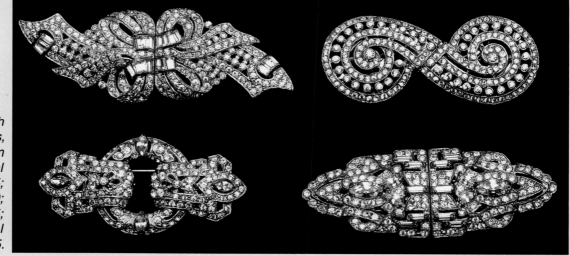

More pieces with clear rhinestones, clockwise from top left: pot metal Clipmate, $155; Coro Duette, $180; Coro Duette, $165; and pot metal Clipmate, $165.

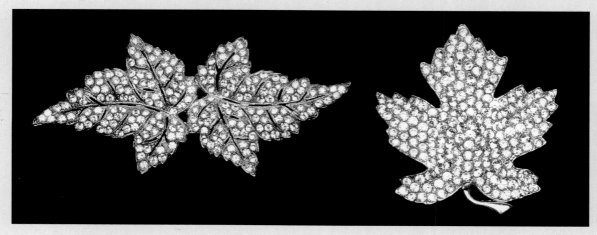

Left: Pot metal double leaf brooch with clear rhinestones, $88. Right: Rhodium leaf brooch with clear rhinestones, $110.

Pot metal pieces, all with clear and red rhinestones, clockwise from top left: brooch, $88; dress clip, $125; dress clip, $32; and bow brooch, $58.

Pot metal bird brooch with clear rhinestones, $195.

An Eisenberg Original leaf brooch with clear rhinestones, $285.

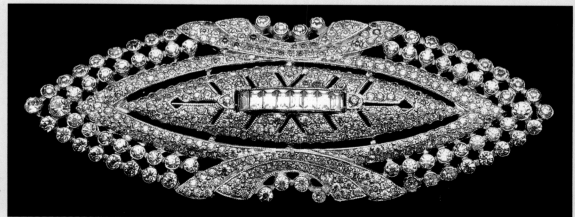

Rhodium Art Deco brooch with clear rhinestones, $148.

An assortment of pot metal and clear rhinestone bird brooches, clockwise from top: $62, $125, $125, and $155 (also has an amethyst rhinestone).

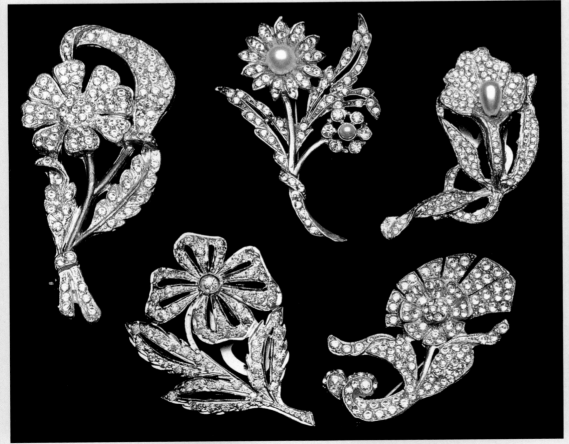

Several floral designs, clockwise from top left: pot metal brooch with clear rhinestones, $72; rhodium brooch with clear rhinestones and faux pearl, $95; pot metal dress clip with clear rhinestones and faux pearl, $46; pot metal brooch with clear rhinestones, $69; and rhodium dress clip with clear rhinestones, $68.

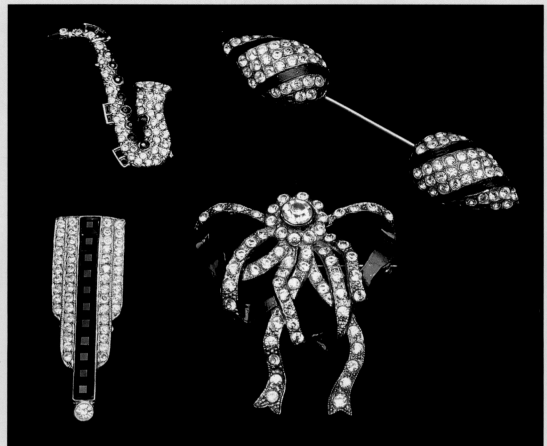

Pot metal pieces, clockwise from top left: saxophone brooch with clear and black rhinestones, $68; double brooch with clear rhinestones and black enameling, $58; bow brooch with clear rhinestones and black enameling, $68; and dress clip with clear and black rhinestones, $48.

Pot metal and clear rhinestone pieces, left to right: brooch, $88; dress clip, $98 (also has blue cabochons); and wheat sheath brooch, $78.

Two Trifari rhodium brooches, both with clear and blue rhinestones and blue enameling, from left: flower, $195, and lily, $355.

Trifari rhodium brooches with clear rhinestones, from left: $140 and $145 (also has light blue open-back rhinestones).

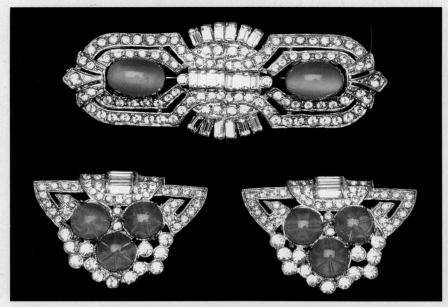

Pot metal pieces, both with clear rhinestones and blue cabochons, from top: Art Deco brooch, $115, and a pair of dress clips, $65.

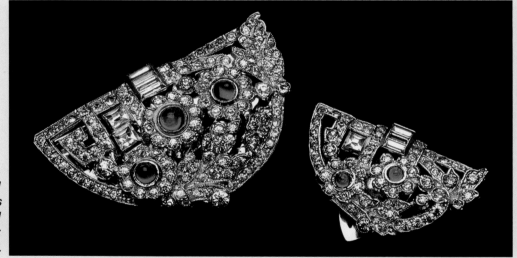

Two pot metal floral design dress clips with clear rhinestones and green cabochons, from left: $98 and $58.

Three-dimensional pot metal bow brooch with clear and blue rhinestones, $158.

Top left and right: Bird fur clips with clear rhinestones and enameling, $125 each. Bottom: Rhodium bird brooch with clear rhinestones and enameling, $110.

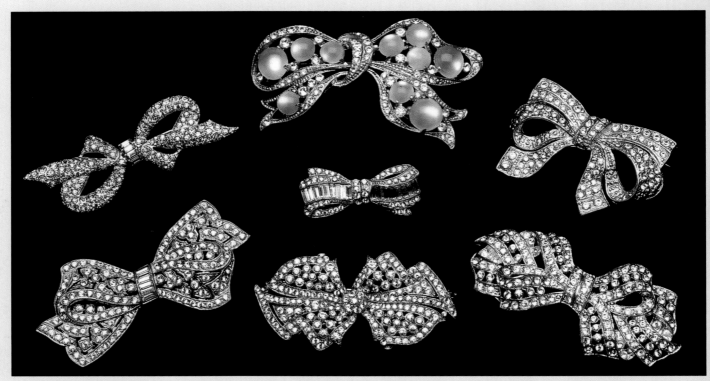

An array of pot metal and clear rhinestone bow brooches, priced clockwise from top left and ending in the center: $68, $110 (also has opalescent cabochons), $85, $98, $188, $135, and $95.

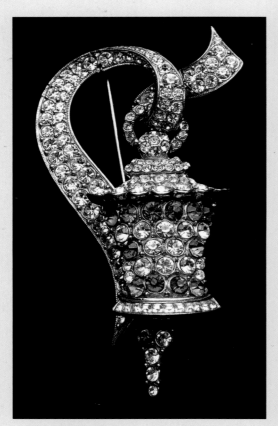

Dangling lantern brooch with clear and green rhinestones set in pot metal, $98.

Sterling horseshoe brooch with floral bouquet, $185.

Floral designs with clear rhinestones and enameling, from left: Mazer brooch, $245, and Trifari fur clip, $195.

Fur clips, from left: grape motif with clear rhinestones, opalescent cabochons, and enameling, $135, and floral design with clear rhinestones, pink cabochons, and enameling, $145.

Several pot metal floral brooches, from left: three-dimensional with clear, amethyst, blue, green, topaz, and pink rhinestones and enameling, $175; with clear rhinestones and green enameling, $110; lily with clear rhinestones and faux pearl, $115; and lily with clear rhinestones and tremblant center, $125.

Pot metal items, from left: floral brooch with red, green, and topaz rhinestones and enameling, $55; tree brooch with clear rhinestones, pink cabochons, and enameling, $85; floral dress clip with clear rhinestones and enameling, $48; and floral brooch with green rhinestones and enameling, $72.

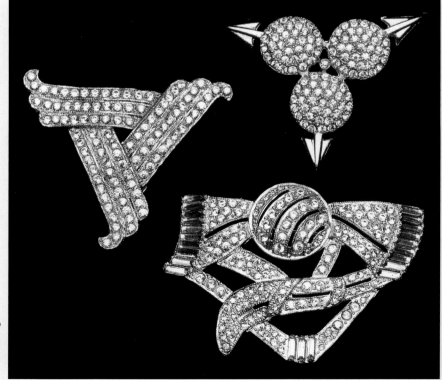

Pot metal and clear rhinestone pieces, clockwise from left: dress clip, $98; brooch, $68; and Art Deco brooch, $135.

Pot metal and clear rhinestone dress clips, from left: $96, $52 (also has light blue rhinestones), and $30.

Pot metal fur clips, left to right: bird with clear, pink, and light blue rhinestones, faux pearl, and enameling, $110; flamingo with clear rhinestones and enameling, $145; and Swiss man with clear rhinestones and enameling, $145.

Sterling silver snake upper-arm bracelet with clear and green rhinestones, $185.

Pot metal bangles, left to right: with blue rhinestones, $66; hinged with blue and clear rhinestones, $68; and hinged with clear and blue rhinestones, $115.

Filigree bangles, from left: with amethyst rhinestones, $145; with blue rhinestone, $110; with green and clear rhinestones, $165; and with clear and blue rhinestones, $115.

Three bracelets, top to bottom: sterling with green and clear rhinestones, $255; sterling link with clear and blue rhinestones, $165; and rhodium with green and blue rhinestones, $225.

Bangles, from left: rhodium hinged with black rhinestones, $145, and filigree buckle with clear rhinestones, $115.

Pot metal and clear rhinestone necklace, $165.

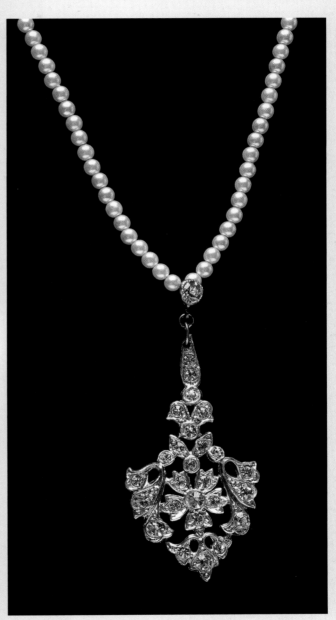

Pot metal and clear rhinestone pendant on faux pearl necklace, $165.

Sterling necklace
with clear rhinestones and cameo, $395.

Sterling silver Art Deco pendant
with marcasites and topaz glass, $385.

Pot metal bow necklace with clear and
black rhinestones, and pendant set on Bakelite, $165.

Clear rhinestone brooches, clockwise from top: circular sterling, $85; Ora pot metal religious motif, $34; pot metal "Taft" style, $42; and pot metal circular with horse, $48.

Sterling necklace with clear rhinestones, $168.

Clear rhinestone pieces, from top:
pot metal bracelet, $115;
Pennino floral bracelet, $145;
and rhodium leaf brooch, $88.

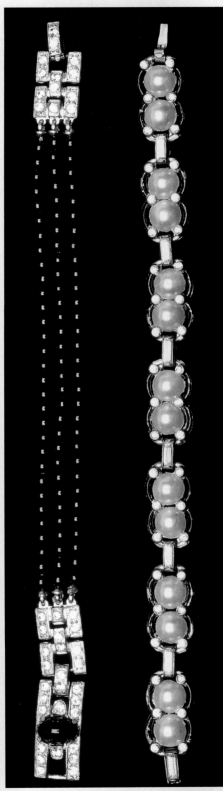

Two pot metal bracelets, from left: with clear rhinestones, black cabochon, and black beads, $110, and with clear rhinestones, faux pearls, and enameling, $98.

Filigree necklace with clear rhinestones and faceted glass, $185.

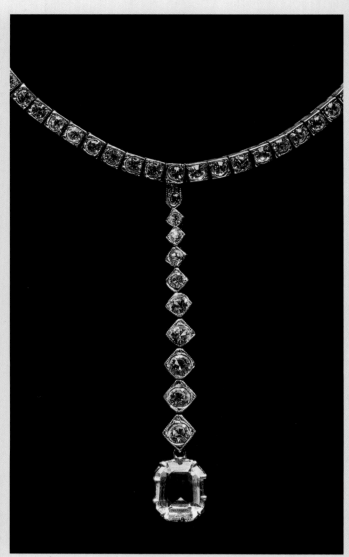

Sterling necklace with clear rhinestones, $385.

Sterling bow necklace with clear rhinestones, $345.

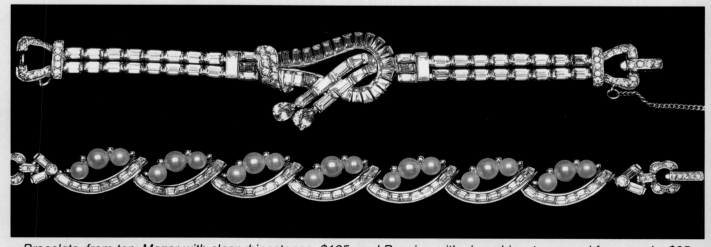

Bracelets, from top: Mazer with clear rhinestones, $185, and Pennino with clear rhinestones and faux pearls, $95.

Pot metal brooches, all with clear rhinestones and enameling, from left: eagle, $185; bird, $125; and Scottie dog, $135 (also has red rhinestones).

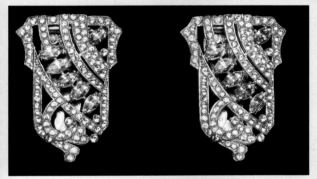

Pair of pot metal dress clips with clear rhinestones, $145.

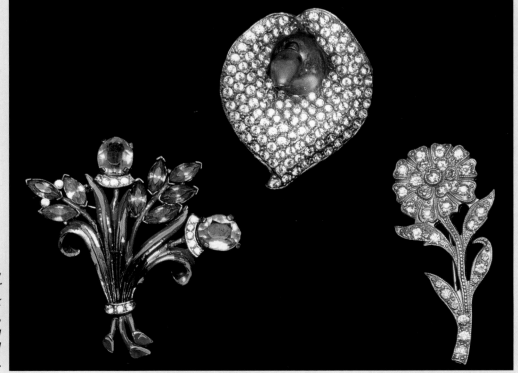

Pot metal floral designs, left to right: brooch with clear rhinestones, blue open-back rhinestones, and enameling, $125; brooch with trembling faux pearl stamen, $135; and pin with clear rhinestones, $48.

Sterling floral design necklace with clear rhinestones, $495.

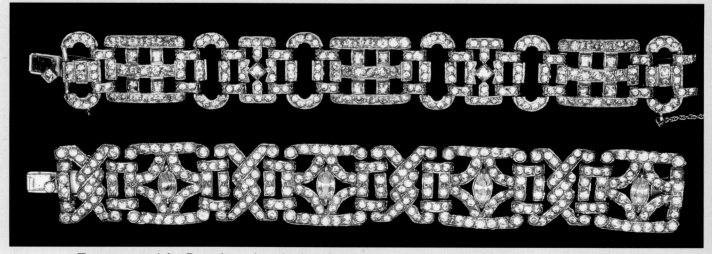

Two pot metal Art Deco bracelets, both with clear rhinestones, priced from top: $195 and $245.

Assorted bracelets, from left: pot metal buckle with clear and red rhinestones, $185; sterling with blue, clear, and red rhinestones, $185; Trifari with red and clear rhinestones along with red and blue cabochons, $245; and sterling with red and clear rhinestones, $168.

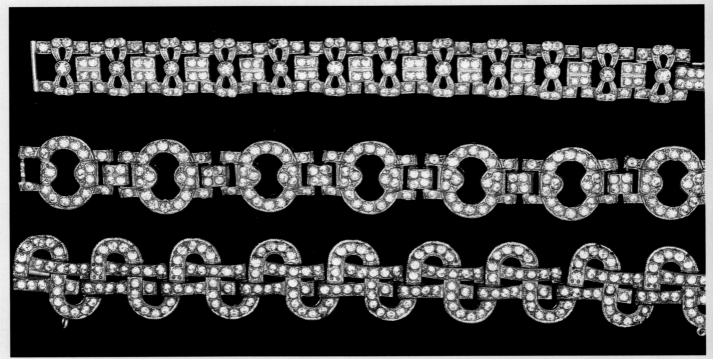

Pot metal and clear rhinestone bracelets, from top: bow design, $140, Art Deco, $185; and Art Deco, $198.

*Pot metal and clear rhinestone buckles,
from top: $65 (in original box) and $45.*

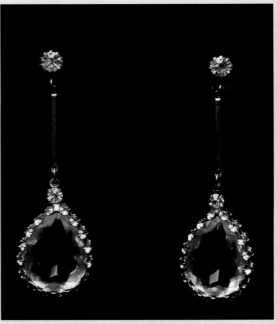

*Pot metal drop-style earrings with
clear rhinestones and faceted glass, $110.*

Pot metal Art Deco earrings
with clear rhinestones, $98.

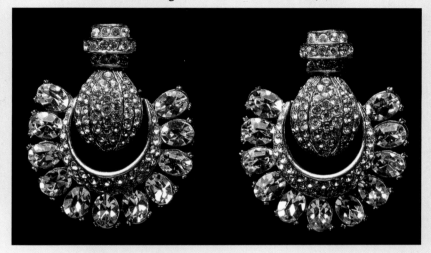

Rhodium earrings with clear rhinestones, $185.

Clear rhinestone earrings, clockwise from top left: Pennino, $85 (also has blue rhinestones);
Wiesner, $65; Jomaz floral, $56; and pot metal, $42.

*Reja brooch and earring set
with clear and open-back rhinestones, $195.*

*Reja brooch and earring set
with clear and open-back rhinestones, $195.*

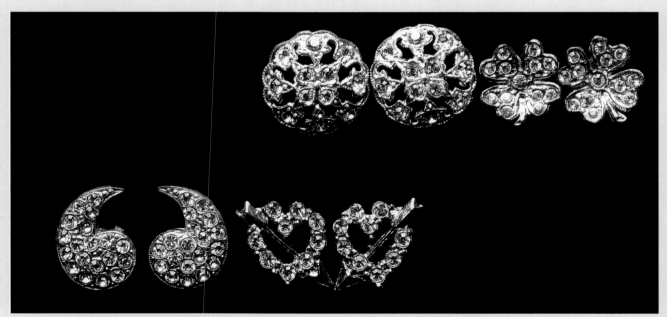

*Four pairs pot metal earrings, all with clear rhinestones, clockwise from top left: circular motif, $36;
four-leaf clover design, $36; Nemo heart and arrow, $28; and apostrophe-like design, $38.*

Clear rhinestone dress clips, clockwise from top left: Trifari, $75; rhodium Art Deco, $85; and a pair of pot metal, $110.

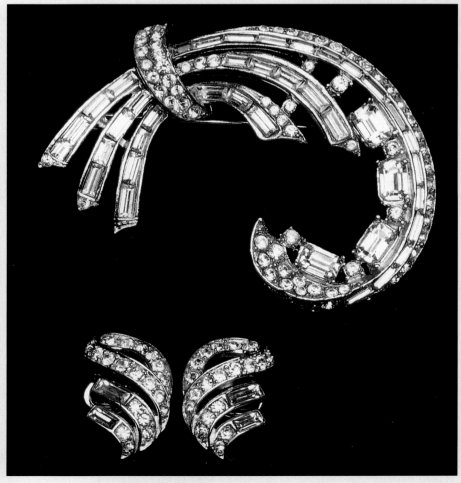

Trifari brooch and earring set with clear rhinestones, $175.

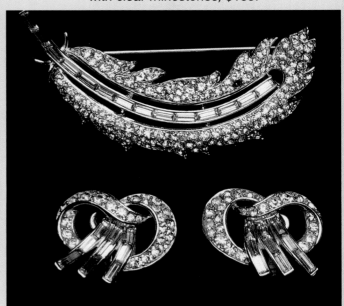

*Trifari brooch and earring set
with clear rhinestones, $135.*

*Eisenberg brooch and earring set
with clear rhinestones, $325.*

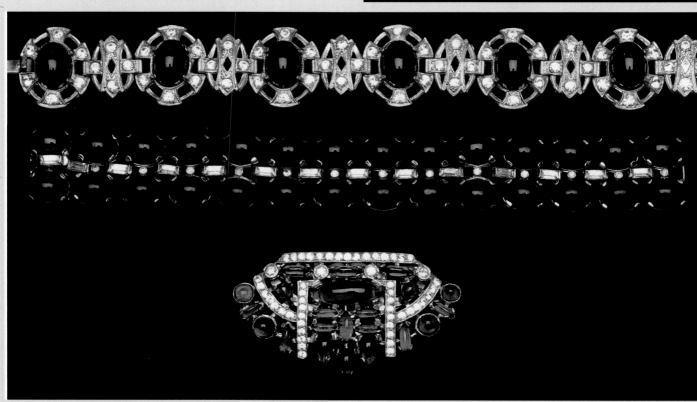

*Three pieces featuring clear rhinestones and green cabochons, top to bottom:
pot metal bracelet, $135; Trifari sterling bracelet, $195; and pot metal dress clip, $98.*

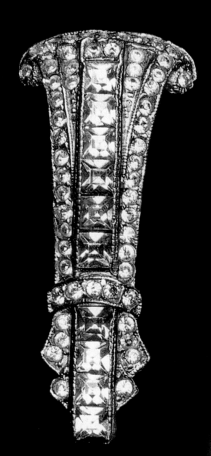

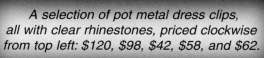
*A selection of pot metal dress clips,
all with clear rhinestones, priced clockwise
from top left: $120, $98, $42, $58, and $62.*

Sterling floral brooch with pink, topaz, and light blue faceted glass, $245.

Clear rhinestone Reja pieces, clockwise from left: bracelet, $145; acorn design brooch, $165; floral design brooch, $165; and earrings, $75.

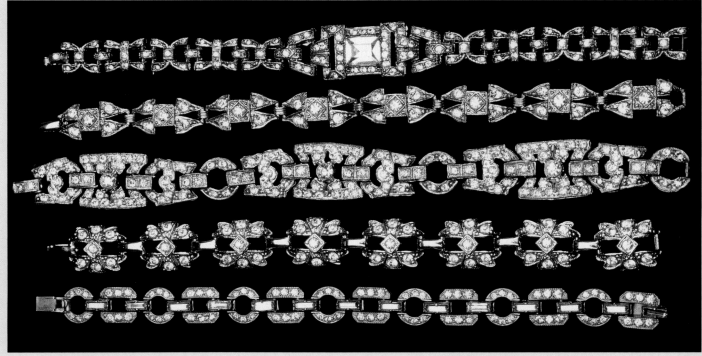

A selection of pot metal bracelets, all with clear rhinestones, priced from top: $110 (also contains faceted glass), $88, $58, $135, and $110.

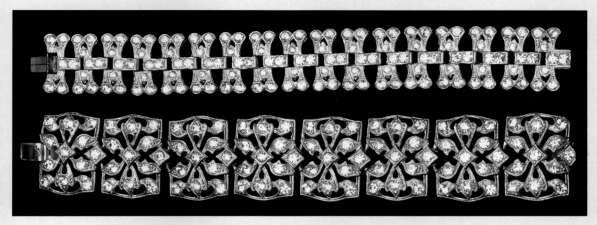

Pot metal and clear rhinestone bracelets, from top: $165 and $145.

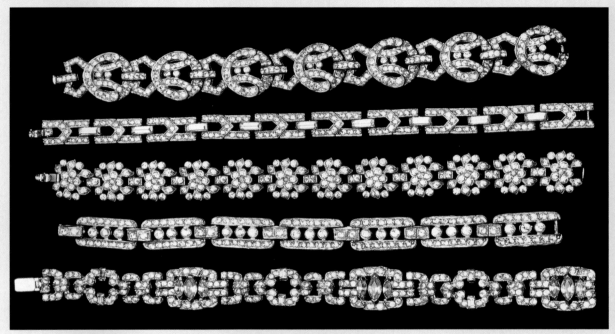

Bracelets with clear rhinestones, from top: sterling, $325; pot metal, $165; pot metal floral design, $195; pot metal $148; and pot metal, $195.

Clockwise from top left: Brooch with clear rhinestones and green cabochon, $86; bow brooch with moveable parts and clear and green rhinestones, $148; and floral dress clip with clear and green rhinestones, $98.

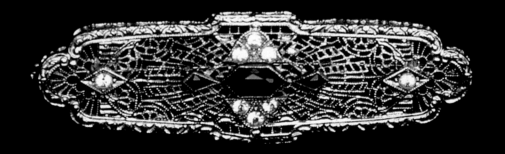

Filigree pieces, from top to bottom: necklace with clear rhinestones, $148; bar pin with clear and green rhinestones, $98; (left) brooch with clear and green rhinestones, $98; (right) brooch with clear rhinestone, $85; and brooch with blue and clear rhinestones, $125.

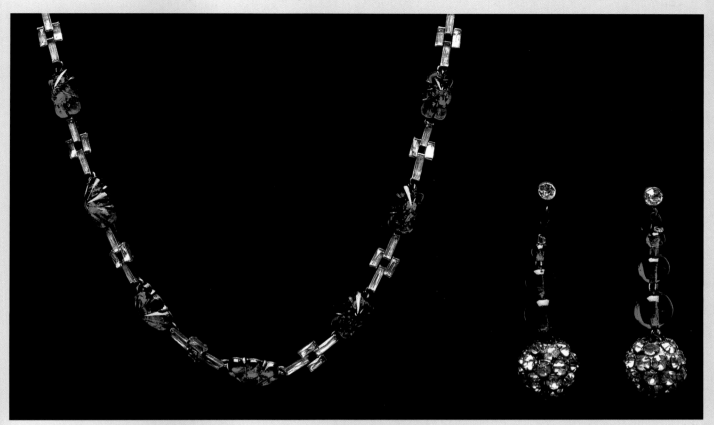

Sterling pieces, from left: necklace with clear rhinestones and molded glass, $165, and earrings with clear rhinestones and green glass beads, $88.

Pell necklace and earring set with clear rhinestones, $210.

A selection of rings, left to right: pot metal with clear and blue rhinestones, $85; rhodium with clear and blue rhinestones, $95; sterling with clear rhinestones and molded glass, $98; sterling with clear rhinestones, $95; and sterling with clear rhinestones, $85.

Two pot metal scarf-holder brooches, from top: with hinged opening for the scarf and clear, red, blue, and green rhinestones, $110, and floral design with hinged opening for the scarf and clear rhinestones, $95.

Flower brooches, from left: pot metal with light blue rhinestones, $125, and rhodium with clear and light blue rhinestones, $168.

Left and right: Pair of pot metal flower brooches with clear rhinestones, $158 each.
Middle: Pot metal flower brooch with clear rhinestones and red cabochons, $165.

Pot metal floral brooches, all with clear rhinestones, priced from left: $178, $195, and $95.

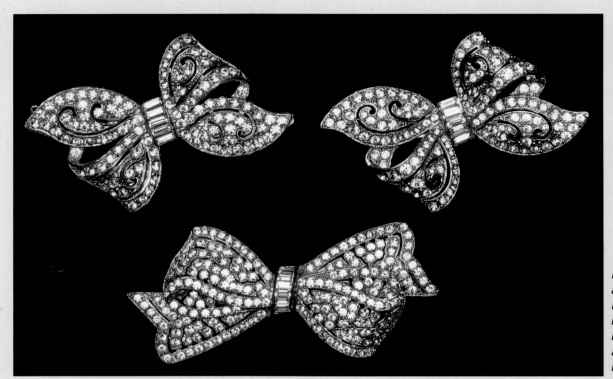

Pot metal and clear rhinestone bow brooches: top, both $125 apiece and bottom, $145.

An array of bow brooches, all with clear rhinestones, clockwise from top: sterling, $285; pot metal, $155; and rhodium, $135.

Bracelets, from left: pot metal with clear rhinestones and green cabochons, $165; sterling with clear and green rhinestones, $135; rhodium with clear and green rhinestones, $225; and another rhodium with clear and green rhinestones, $225.

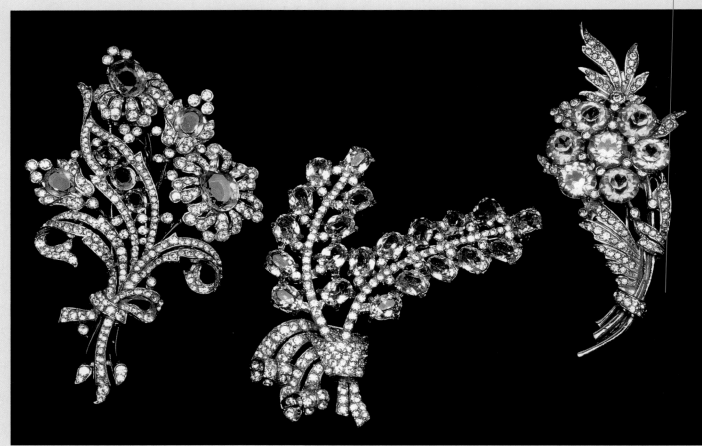

Floral designs, left to right: Trifari rhodium fur clip with clear rhinestones, green open-back rhinestones, and enameling, $395; pot metal brooch with clear rhinestones and clear open-back rhinestones, $165; and rhodium brooch with clear rhinestones and yellow open-back rhinestones, $185.

Pot metal brooches, from left: bow with clear rhinestones, $185, and question mark, $95.

Floral brooches, clockwise from top: pot metal with clear rhinestones and molded glass, $110; Reinad rhodium with clear rhinestones and amethyst faceted glass, $395; and rhodium with clear rhinestones and amethyst open-back rhinestones, $185.

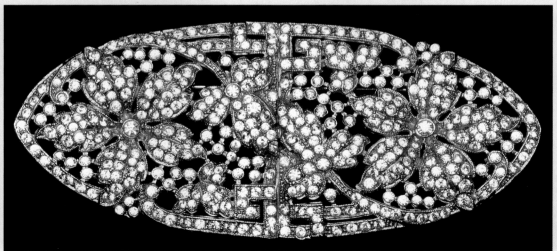

Pot metal floral brooch with clear rhinestones, $495.

Left top and bottom: Identical pot metal flower brooches with clear rhinestones, $155 each.
Right: Artisan NY pot metal flower brooch with clear rhinestones and faux pearls, $165.

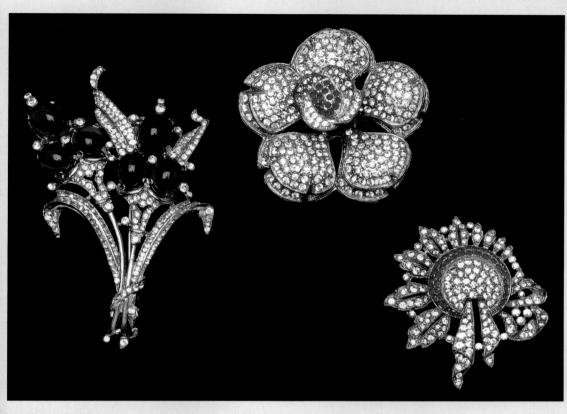

Floral brooches, left to right: rhodium with clear rhinestones and red cabochons, $265; pot metal trembler with clear and red rhinestones, $195; and rhodium with clear and red rhinestones, $95.

A selection of pot metal brooches, all with clear rhinestones, priced clockwise from top left and ending in the middle: $90, $110, $168 (also has enameling), $95, and $78.

Pot metal floral brooches, clockwise from top left: with clear and amethyst rhinestones, $185; with clear and green rhinestones, $210; and trembler with clear and green rhinestones and enameling, $185.

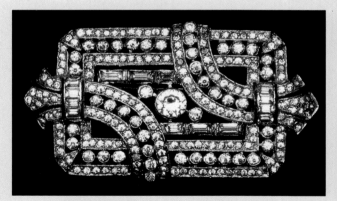

TKF rhodium Art Deco brooch, $175.

Two flower brooches, both with three-dimensional stamens and clear rhinestones, from left: pot metal, $185, and rhodium, $265.

Flower trembler brooches, all with clear rhinestones, left to right:
Staret, $395; pot metal, $95 (also has blue rhinestones); and pot metal, $135.

Three pot metal bow brooches, all with clear rhinestones, priced clockwise from top: $145 (also has blue rhinestones), $145, and $85.

Pot metal brooches, clockwise from top: grape design with clear, topaz, red, green, and blue rhinestones, $65; flower with clear, green, red, and blue rhinestones as well as enameling, $88; and bow with light green, blue, topaz, and amethyst rhinestones, $78.

Flower design brooches, all with clear rhinestones, left to right: pot metal, $165; rhodium, $165; pot metal, $35; and pot metal, $210.

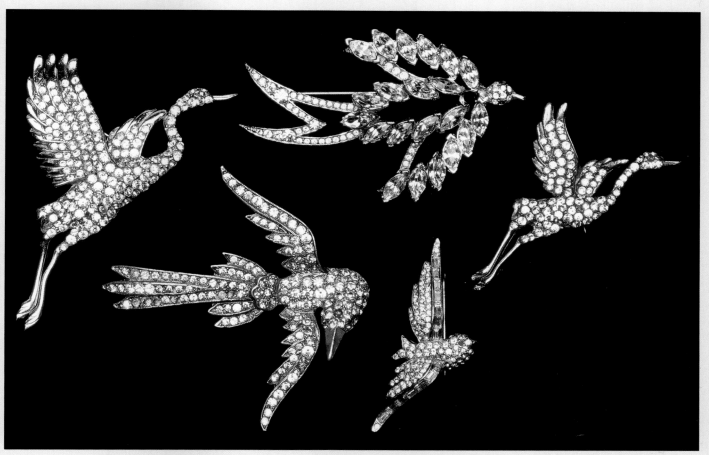

*Bird brooches, clockwise from top left: rhodium with clear and blue rhinestones, $160;
Corocraft with clear and green rhinestones, $110; pot metal with clear and red rhinestones, $98;
Halbe rhodium with clear and red rhinestones, $85; and rhodium with clear rhinestones, $145.*

Two rhodium floral brooches, from left: with clear and blue rhinestones, $188, and with clear rhinestones and blue cabochons, $155.

Sterling Art Deco necklace with clear and blue rhinestones and faceted blue glass, $245.

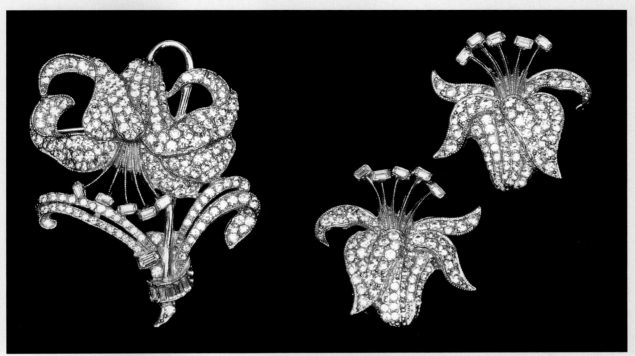

Ora floral brooch and matching earrings with clear rhinestones, $195.

Brooches, clockwise from top left: pot metal concentric circle with clear, topaz, and green rhinestones, $135; rhodium with clear and pink rhinestones, $145; pot metal with clear and green rhinestones, $235; and rhodium with clear and green rhinestones, $130.

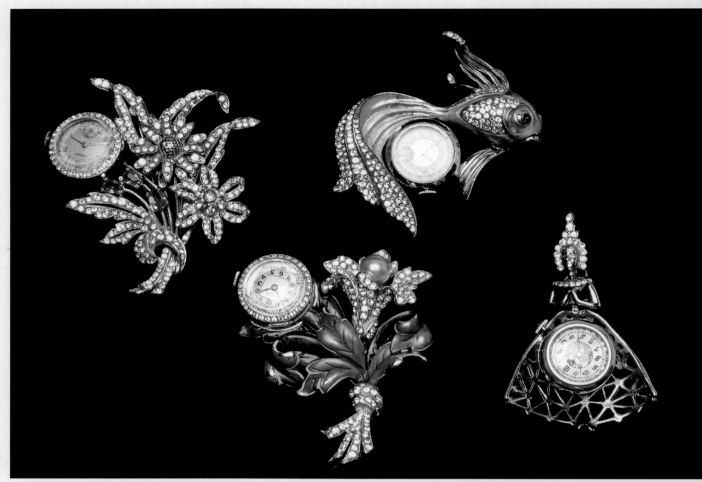

Brooches, clockwise from top left: rotary floral with watch, clear and blue rhinestones, $385;
Harvel fish with watch, clear rhinestones, green cabochons and enameling, $395;
woman with watch and clear, blue, red, and green rhinestones as well as enameling, $345;
and Pierce floral with watch, clear rhinestones, faux pearls, and enameling, $465.

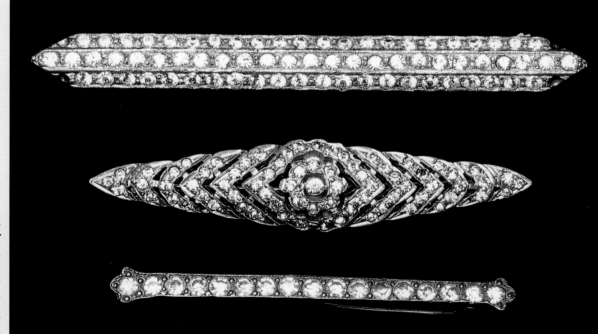

Bar pins,
all with clear
rhinestones,
top to bottom:
pot metal, $58;
rhodium, $85;
and pot metal,
$28.

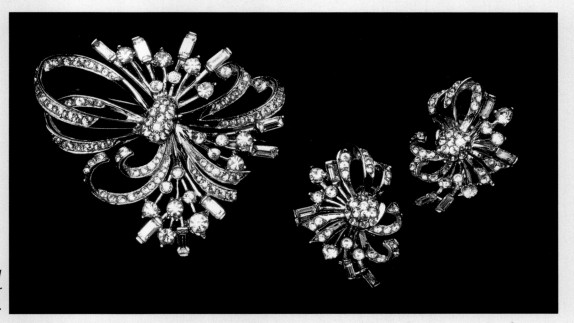

Boucher brooch and earrings with clear rhinestones, $285.

Sterling crown brooch and matching earrings with clear rhinestones, $245.

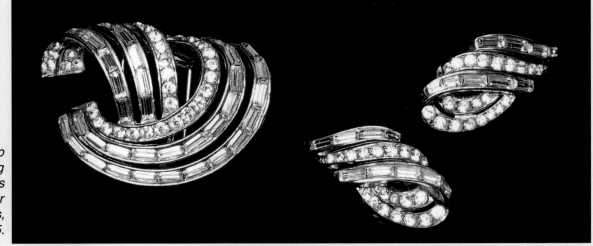

Boucher fur clip and matching earrings with clear rhinestones, $175.

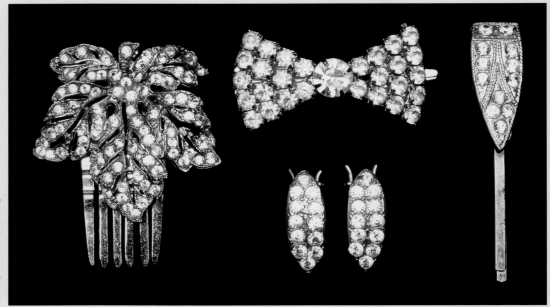

Pot metal and clear rhinestone pieces, clockwise from left: hair clip, $48; bow hair clip, $36; bobby pin, $18; and a pair of hair clips, $38.

An assortment of brooches, left to right: (top row) pot metal with clear rhinestones, $32; pot metal with clear and green rhinestones, $55; pot metal with clear rhinestones, $38; (middle) pot metal with clear rhinestones, $42; sterling circular with clear and green rhinestones, $60; pot metal with clear rhinestones and enameling, $48; (bottom) pot metal with clear and blue rhinestones, $65; and pot metal with clear and red rhinestones, $38.

Pot metal and clear rhinestone pieces, from left: floral design necklace, $245, and earrings, $110.

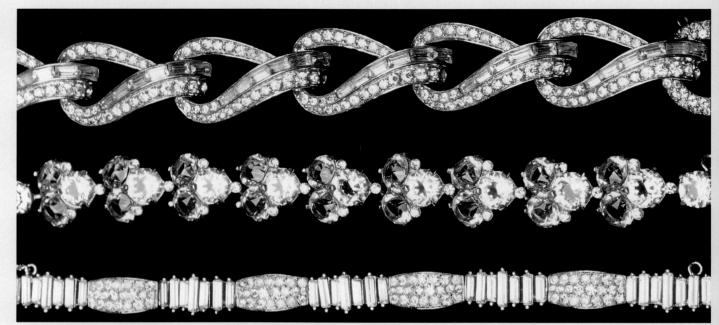

Rhodium bracelets, all with clear rhinestones, from top: unsigned, $165; Reja, $195; and Trifari, $185.

Sterling bracelets, from top: unsigned with clear rhinestones, $185; Otis with clear rhinestones, $265; and Payco bracelet with clear and light blue rhinestones, $225.

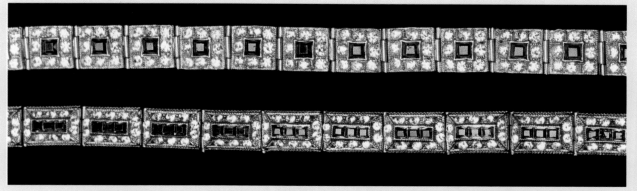

Two more bracelets, from top: Diamond Bar with clear and sapphire rhinestones, $275, and pot metal with clear and amethyst rhinestones, $225.

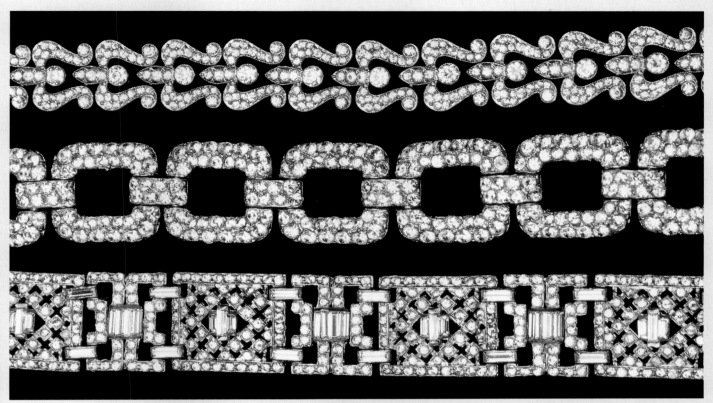

Clear rhinestone bracelets, from top: rhodium, $245; pot metal, $225; and rhodium, $345.

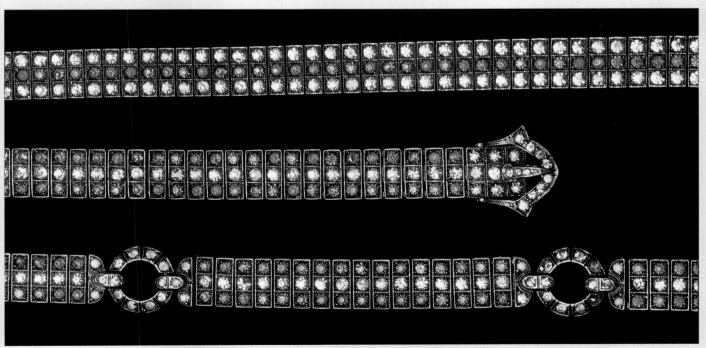

Three sterling Diamond Bar bracelets, all with clear and blue rhinestones, priced top to bottom: $295, $285 (also has buckle), and $245.

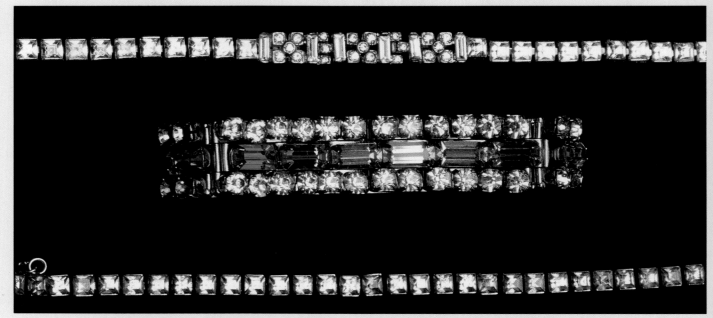

A trio of bracelets, from top: Ledo with clear rhinestones, $110; expandable with clear and light blue rhinestones, $110; and rhodium with light blue rhinestones, $80.

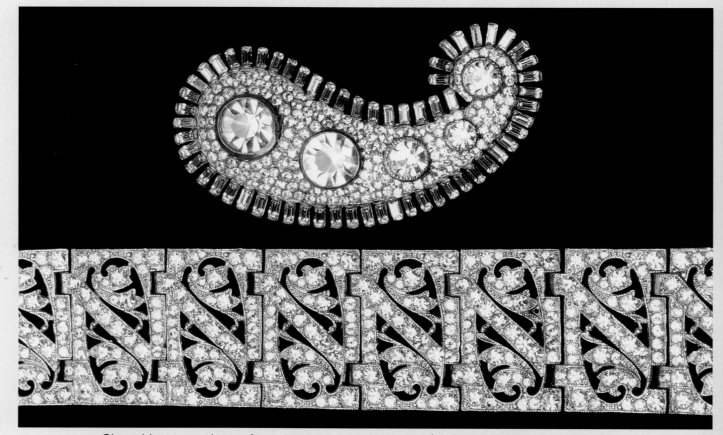

Clear rhinestone pieces, from top: pot metal dress clip, $195, and rhodium bracelet, $425.

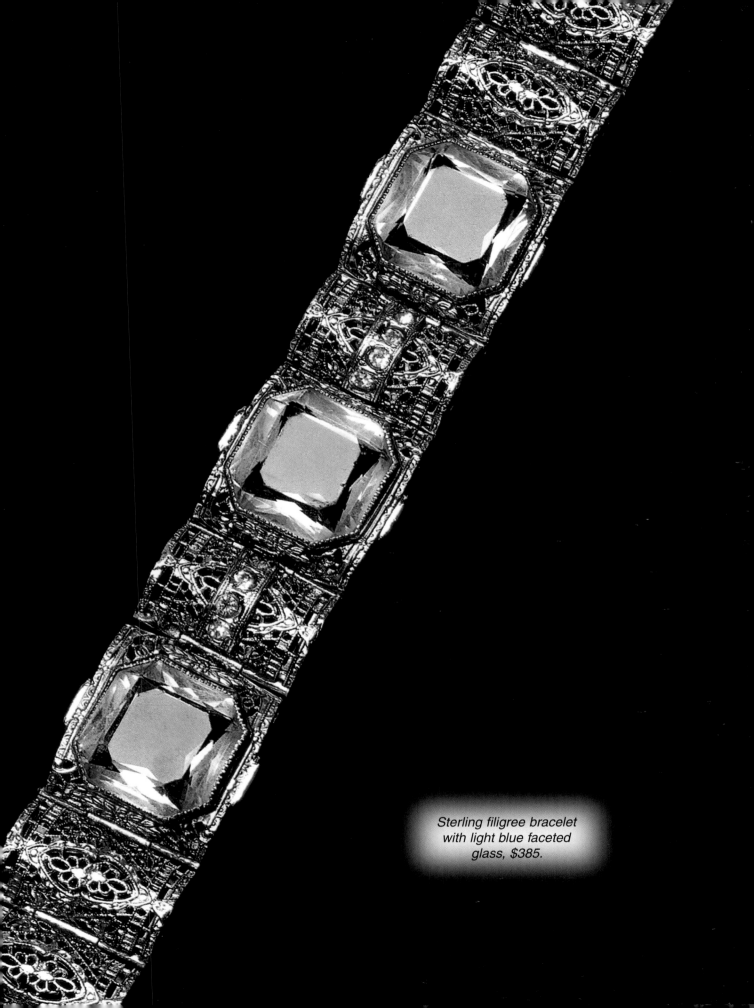

Sterling filigree bracelet with light blue faceted glass, $385.

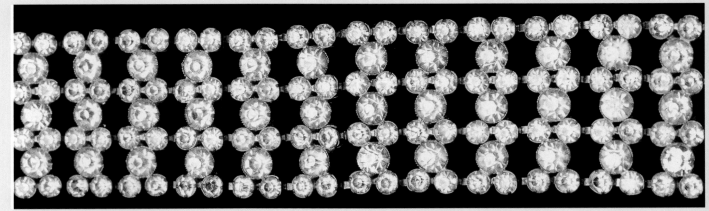

Czechoslovakian bracelet with clear rhinestones, $195.

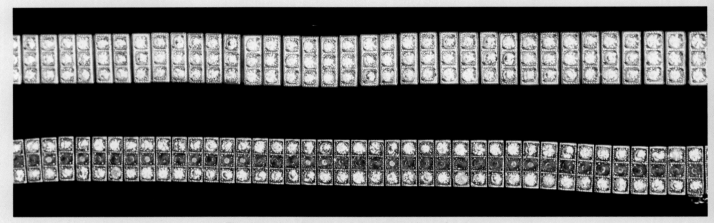

Two sterling Diamond Bar bracelets, from top:
with buckle and clear rhinestones, $275, and with clear and red rhinestones, $245.

Bracelets, all with clear and green rhinestones, from top: rhodium, $245; pot metal, $265; and ALL Co., $295.

*Flower brooches,
all with clear rhinestones,
clockwise from top left:
pot metal, $185;
pot metal, $110;
and rhodium, $165.*

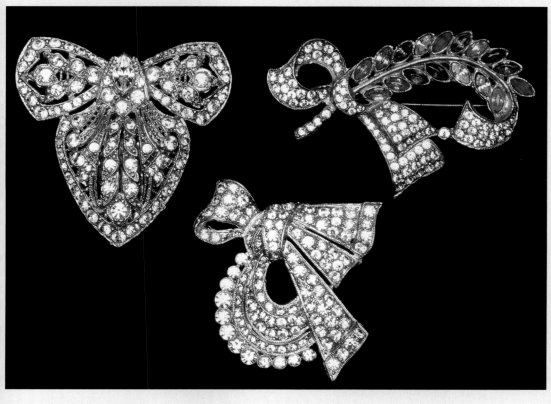

*Pot metal pieces,
clockwise from top left:
bow dress clip with
clear rhinestones, $65;
brooch with clear, red,
green, blue, topaz,
lavender, and light blue
rhinestones, $84;
and bow brooch with
clear rhinestones, $62.*

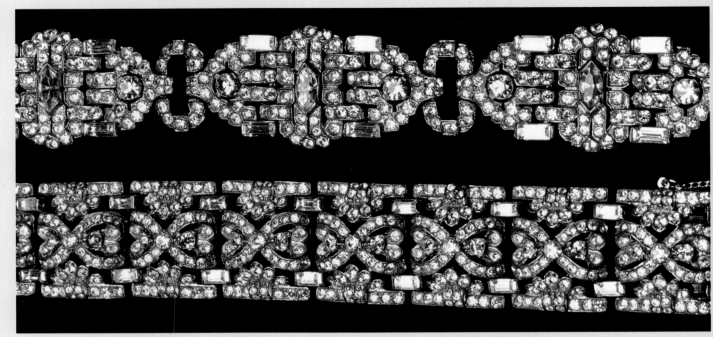

Two clear rhinestone bracelets, from top: pot metal, $245, and rhodium, $395.

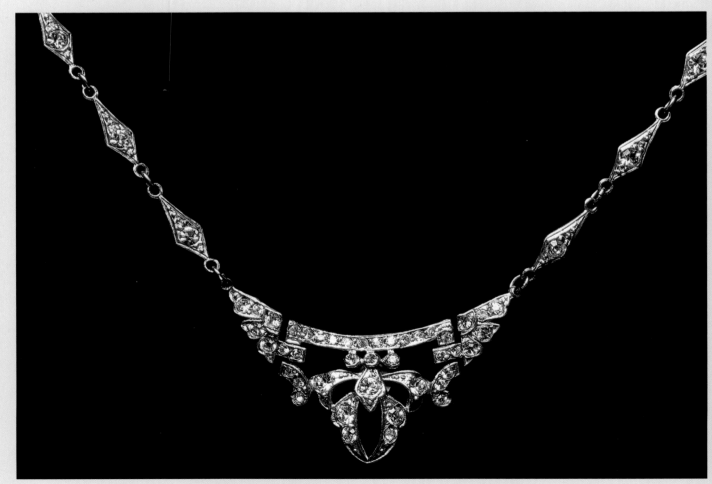

Pot metal necklace with clear rhinestones, $145.

Rhodium flower brooch with clear rhinestones, $495.

Dress clips, left to right: rhodium floral with clear rhinestones and enameling, $65; pot metal with clear rhinestones and molded glass, $58; and pot metal with clear rhinestones, pink, light blue, yellow, and green cabochons and enameling, $46.

Pot metal floral brooches, left to right: with pink open-back rhinestones and enameling, $82; with clear rhinestones and enameling, $95; and Coro with topaz rhinestones and enameling, $88.

Sterling necklace with clear rhinestones and pink faceted glass, $245.

Sterling Art Deco pendant with clear rhinestones,
faceted glass, and enameling, $395.

Pot metal necklace with clear rhinestones, $180.

Rhodium necklace with clear rhinestones and faceted glass, $185.

Pot metal necklace with clear rhinestones, $95.

Necklaces, from top: pot metal Art Deco with clear and green rhinestones, $195, and sterling with clear rhinestones and green faceted glass, $185.

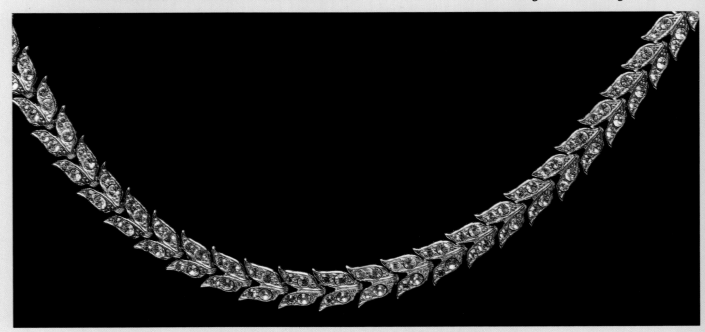

Rhodium necklace with clear rhinestones, $165.

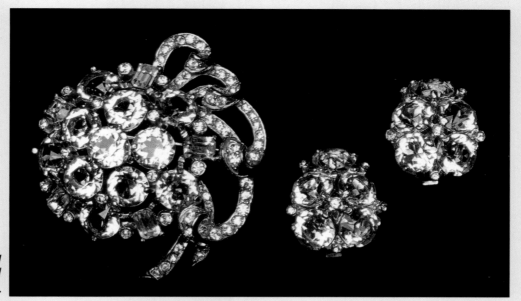

Reja brooch and matching earrings with clear and open-back rhinestones, $195.

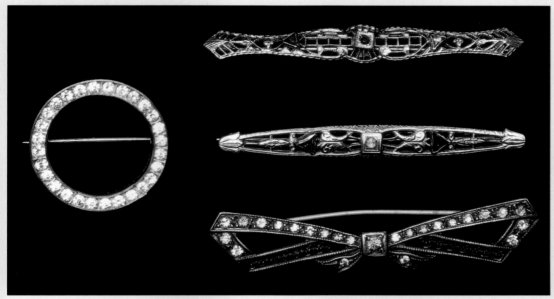

Pins, clockwise from left: sterling circular pin with clear rhinestones, $62; filigree bar with clear and red rhinestones, $65; filigree bar with clear and blue rhinestones, $85; and sterling bow with clear rhinestones, $95.

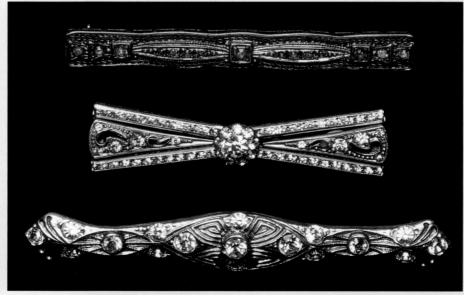

Clear rhinestone bar pins, from top: sterling, $90; sterling Art Deco, $125; and pot metal, $90.

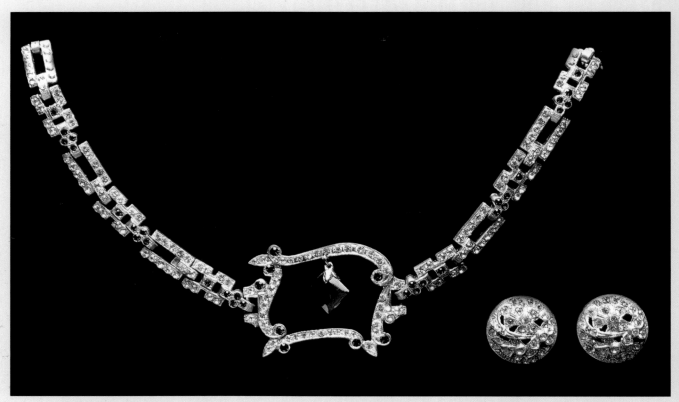

Pot metal, from left: necklace with clear and green rhinestones and green faceted glass, $195, and earrings with clear rhinestones, $45.

Pot metal and clear rhinestone pieces, from left: necklace, $145, and floral earrings, $88.

Counterclockwise from top: Pot metal pendant with clear rhinestones and red, blue, and green cabochons, $110; pot metal necklace with clear rhinestones and blue faceted glass, $165; and sterling earrings with clear rhinestones, $65.

Sterling earrings with clear rhinestones and red faceted glass, $295.

Sterling earrings with clear rhinestones and faceted glass, $115.

Pot metal necklace and earrings, both with clear rhinestones: $195 and $95.

Pot metal earrings with clear rhinestones
and faux pearls, $135.

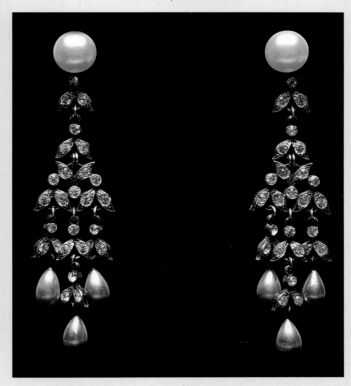

Sterling earrings with clear rhinestones
and faux pearls, $165.

Clear rhinestone earrings, from left: wingback, $65, and pot metal, $72 (also has faux pearls).

Earrings, counterclockwise from top left: sterling with clear rhinestones and blue faceted glass, $145; Boucher with clear rhinestones and blue cabochons, $65; and sterling with light blue rhinestones, $45.

Pot metal earrings with clear rhinestones, $110.

Sterling earrings with clear rhinestones, $185.

Four pairs rhodium earrings, from left: with clear and red rhinestones, $75; with clear rhinestones, $65; another with clear rhinestones, $125; with clear rhinestones and green cabochons, $65.

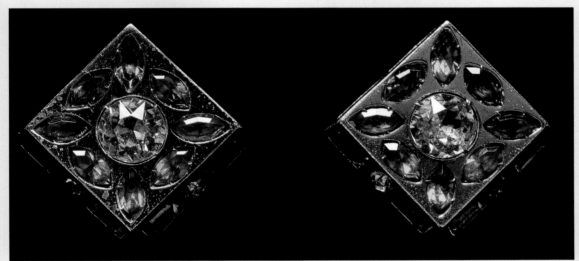

Rhodium earrings with clear and topaz rhinestones, $45.

Earring pairs, all with clear rhinestones and faux pearls, left to right: rhodium, $62; pot metal, $52; and Mazer rhodium, $75.

*Clear rhinestone earrings, from left: sterling BB horseshoe, $60;
pot metal, $45; pot metal pair, $42; and rhodium, $72.*

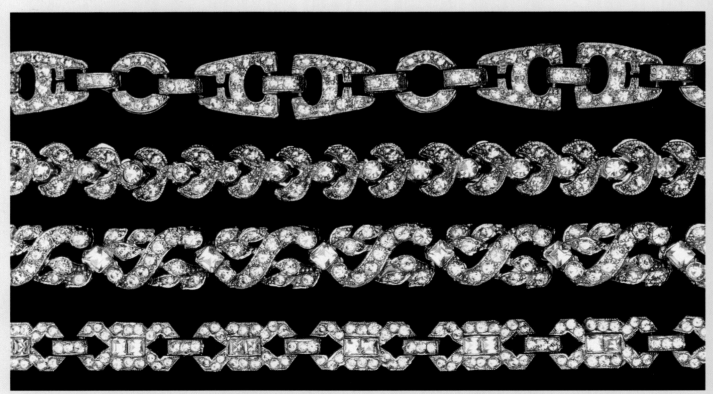

A selection of pot metal bracelets, all with clear rhinestones, priced top to bottom: $165, $145, $145, and $140.

Top: Rhodium necklace with clear rhinestones and green faceted glass, $395. Bottom: Sterling earrings with clear and green rhinestones, $85.

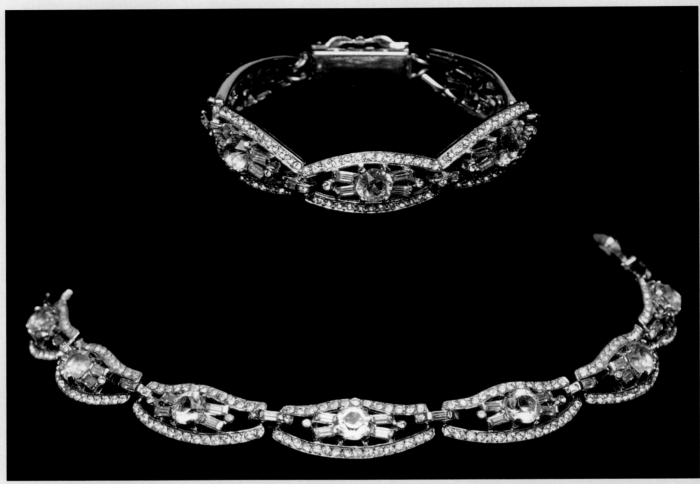

Boucher necklace and matching bracelet with clear and open-back rhinestones and faceted glass, $345.

Bangles, left to right: pot metal with clear and amethyst rhinestones, $185;
pot metal hinged with clear rhinestones, $165; and sterling hinged double row with clear rhinestones, $265.

*Two pot metal snake design bracelets, from left: with clear and red rhinestones, $145,
and with light blue and red rhinestones, $145.*

Pot metal star design necklace with clear rhinestones, $185.

Rhodium hinged bangle with clear rhinestones, pink, blue, and green faceted glass, as well as red cabochons, $595.

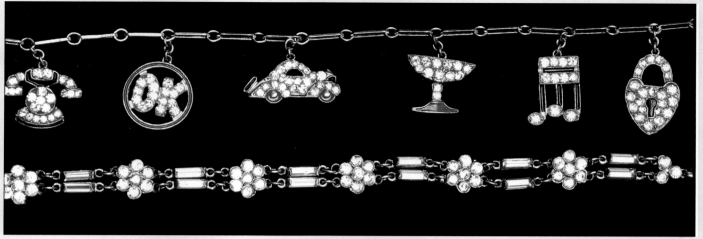

Pot metal bracelets, from top:
charm style with clear rhinestones and enameling, $145, and with clear rhinestones, $98.

More bracelets, from top: rhodium with clear rhinestones, $145; sterling with
clear rhinestones and faceted glass, $185; and sterling with clear rhinestones and faux pearls, $195.

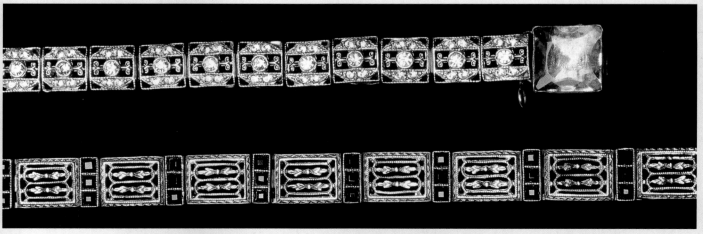

Two sterling bracelets, from top: with clear rhinestones and faceted glass, $295,
and Diamond Bar with black rhinestones, $225.

Bracelets with clear rhinestones, from left: pot metal, $110; sterling, $325 (also has pink cabochons); and pot metal, $155.

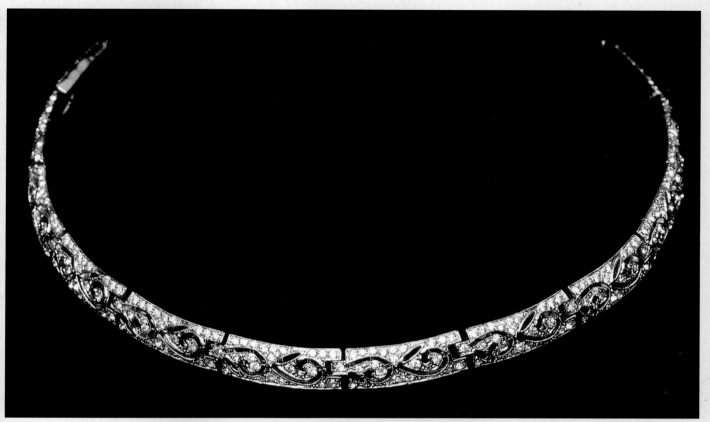

Rhodium necklace with clear rhinestones, $195.

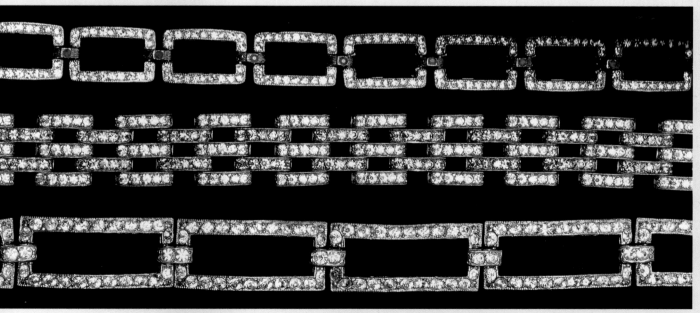

Three bracelets, from top: pot metal with clear and red rhinestones, $125;
rhodium with clear and light blue rhinestones, $225; and pot metal with clear rhinestones, $110.

Butterfly brooches, from left: pot metal with clear and blue rhinestones, $110; pot metal with clear, blue, and red rhinestones, $88; and rhodium with clear rhinestones and red and green cabochons, $185.

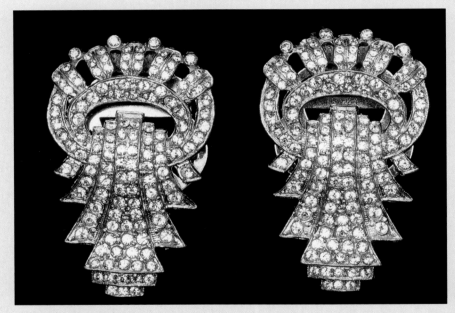

Pair of pot metal dress clips, $145.

Three pot metal brooches, all with clear rhinestones, left to right: bug, $28; floral design, $32; and dog, $48.

Two baubles with clear rhinestones and pink cabochons, from top: sterling bar pin, $95, and rhodium bracelet, $95.

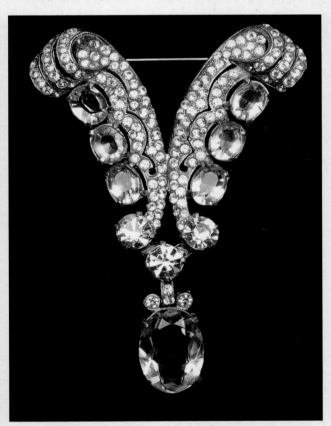

Salvo NYC Art Deco brooch with clear rhinestones and faceted glass, $295.

Left: Pot metal bracelet with clear and black rhinestones, $145. Right: Art Deco necklace with clear and black rhinestones, faux pearls, black glass beads, and clear faceted glass, $245.

Left: Delsa bracelet with clear rhinestones and blue and clear faceted glass, $285. Right: Rhodium flower brooch with clear rhinestones and blue faceted glass, $185.

Pot metal butterfly brooch and matching earrings with clear and green rhinestones, $395.

Clear rhinestones pieces, from left: sterling floral brooch, $185, and rhodium earrings, $62.

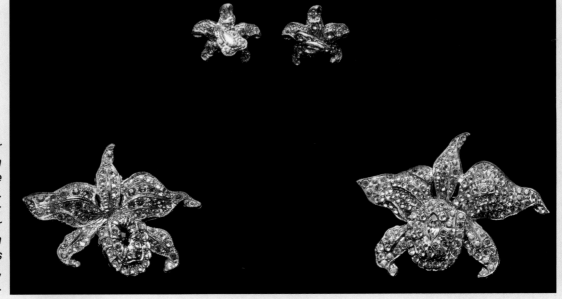

Left: Pot metal flower trembler brooch with clear and blue rhinestones, $125. Right and middle: Pot metal flower trembler brooch and matching earrings with clear rhinestones, $188.

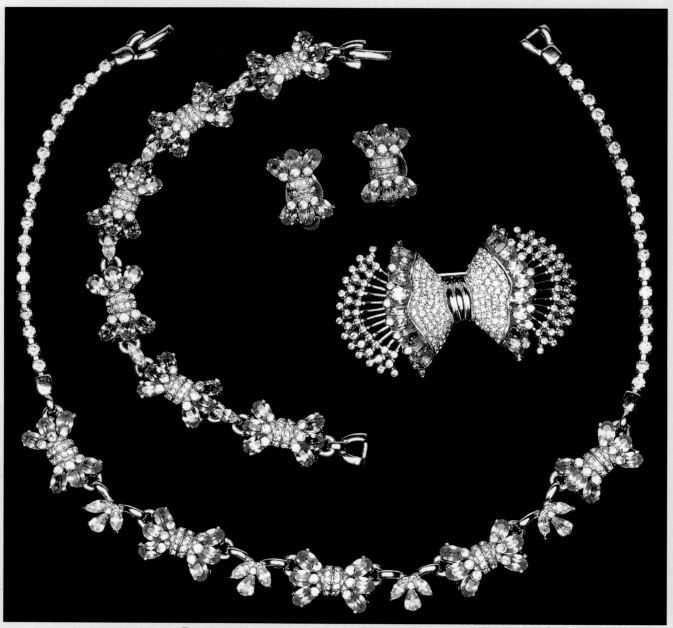

*Pennino necklace, earrings, bracelet, and brooch set
with clear rhinestones and blue open-back rhinestones, $875.*

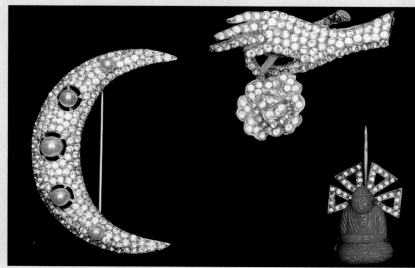

*Clockwise from left: Rhodium moon brooch
with clear rhinestones and faux pearls, $110;
pot metal hand brooch with trembling flower,
clear rhinestones, and enameling, $145;
and sterling Buddha stickpin with
clear rhinestones and molded glass, $85.*

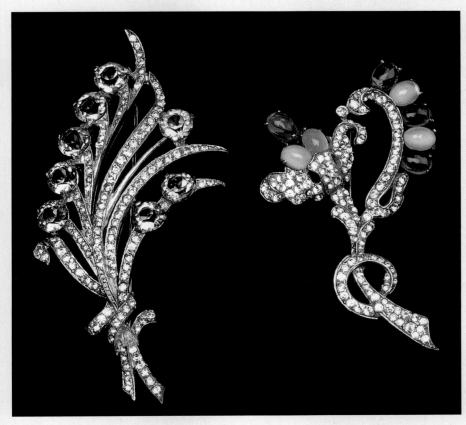

Brooches, from left: rhodium floral
with clear rhinestones and blue
open-back rhinestones, $210,
and sterling with clear rhinestones
and blue cabochons, $245.

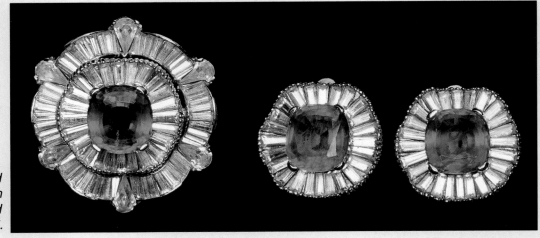

Jomaz brooch and
matching earrings with
clear rhinestones and
green faceted glass, $245.

Left: Boucher brooch
with clear and blue
rhinestones, $185.
Right: Sterling
earrings with
clear rhinestones
and blue open-back
rhinestones, $125.

Two pot metal musical note brooches, from left: with clear and red rhinestones, $118, and with clear rhinestones, $48.

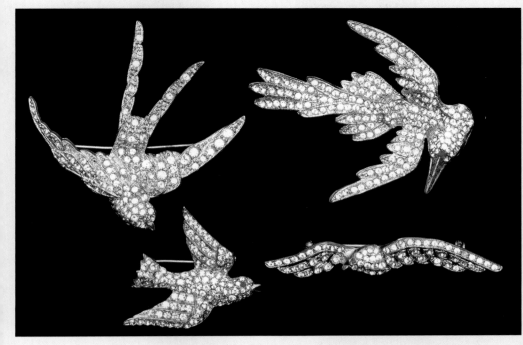

Bird brooches, clockwise from top left: pot metal with clear and blue rhinestones, $98; pot metal with clear and red rhinestones, $145; pot metal with clear and red rhinestones, $88; and Corocraft sterling with clear and red rhinestones, $165.

Marcasite brooches, clockwise from top left: sterling with blue faceted glass, $115; pot metal with blue open-back rhinestones and enameling, $98; and pot metal with blue open-back rhinestones, $155.

Left: Pot metal dragonfly brooch with clear rhinestones and enameling, $165. Right: Sterling bug brooch with clear, red, and green rhinestones and enameling, $185.

*Pot metal floral brooches, from left:
with clear rhinestones, faux pearls,
and enameling, $195, and with clear and
light blue rhinestones and enameling, $115.*

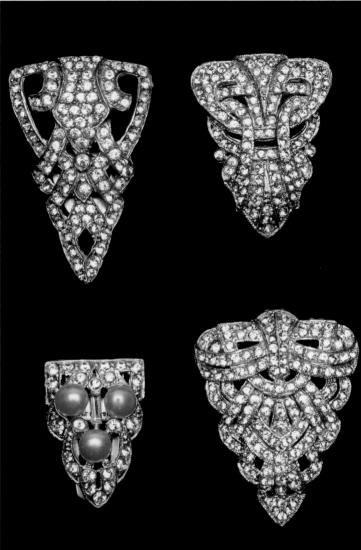

*A selection of pot metal and clear rhinestone dress clips,
priced clockwise from top left: $68, $78, $92,
and $48 (also has faux pearls).*

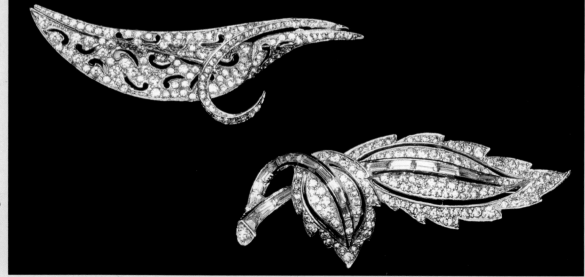

*Clear rhinestone
leaf brooches,
from top:
rhodium, $110,
and Kramer, $110.*

Pot metal brooches, clockwise from top left: three-dimensional fish with clear rhinestones and enameling, $265; fish with clear rhinestones and enameling, $110; stork with clear rhinestones and enameling, $295; and fish with clear rhinestones, blue cabochons, and enameling, $115.

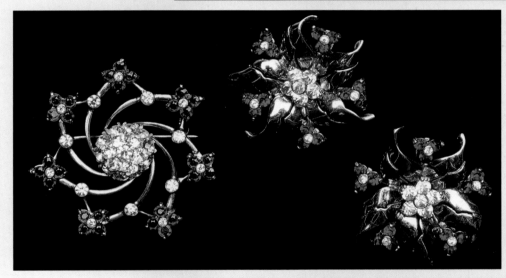

Pennino sterling brooch and matching earrings with clear and green rhinestones, $195.

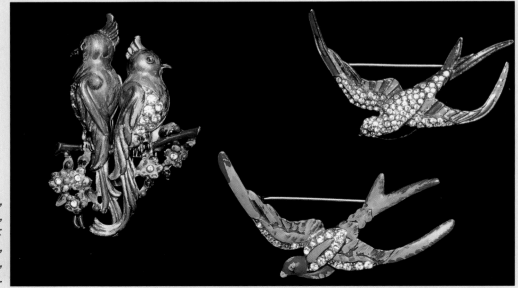

Enameled bird pieces, all with clear rhinestones, clockwise from left: Coro Duette, $145, and two pot metal brooches, $125 and $110.

Pot metal bird brooches, both with clear rhinestones and enameling, priced from left: $98 and $125.

Marcasite brooches,
clockwise from top left:
pot metal with green cabochons, $95;
sterling with enameling, $125; and
sterling ballerina with enameling, $90.

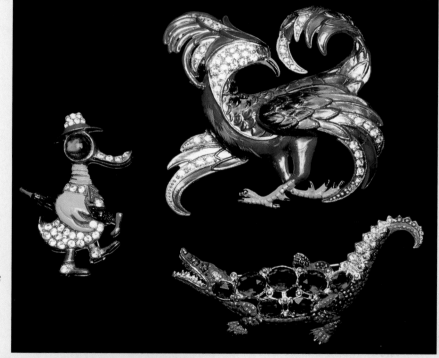

An array of pot metal brooches,
clockwise from left:
duck with clear rhinestones, green
cabochons, and enameling, $110;
bird with clear and red rhinestones
and enameling, $195;
and alligator with clear rhinestones,
green open-back rhinestones,
and enameling, $155.

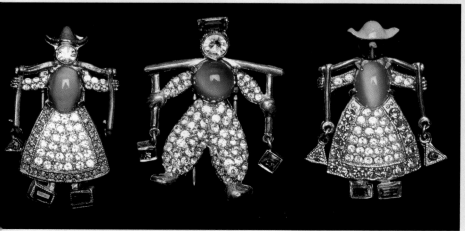

Pot metal fur clips, left to right:
woman with clear, blue, and
black rhinestones and
an amethyst cabochon, $85;
with clear and blue rhinestones
and pink cabochon, $85;
and with clear, blue, amethyst, and
green rhinestones, a pink cabochon,
and enameling, $85.

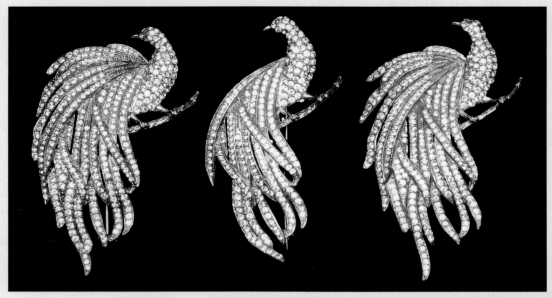

Identical pot metal bird brooches with clear rhinestones, $245 each.

A selection of pot metal and clear rhinestone buckles, priced clockwise from top left: $65, $55, $58, and $45.

Pot metal brooches, all with clear rhinestones and enameling, left to right: stagecoach, $115; airplane, $145; and sailboat, $135.

Bird brooches, clockwise from top left: Silson with clear rhinestones and enameling, $195; Boucher with clear rhinestones, faux pearls, and enameling, $325; and pot metal with clear and pink rhinestones, faux pearls, and enameling, $185.

Pot metal with red, green, blue, and topaz rhinestones, from left: dress clip, $85, and brooch, $95.

Clear rhinestone dress clips, left to right: pot metal, $88; pot metal, $165; and rhodium, $185.

Pot metal animal brooches, clockwise from top left: squirrel with clear rhinestones and enameling, $195; dog with clear rhinestones and molded glass, $185; and turtle with clear and red rhinestones, $135.

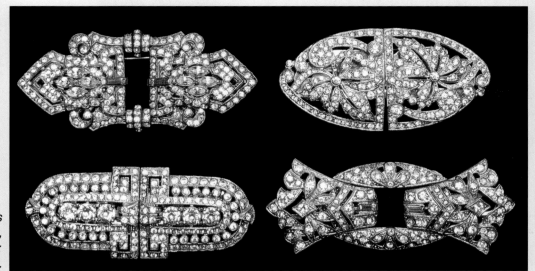

A selection of Duettes with clear rhinestones, priced clockwise from top left: $195, $225, $195, and $172.

Brooches, clockwise from top left: rhodium with clear rhinestones and green cabochons, $98; AJ pot metal with clear rhinestones and green cabochons, $195; and rhodium with clear rhinestones, $165.

Clear rhinestone brooches, from left: rhodium bow, $145, and sterling snowflake, $125.

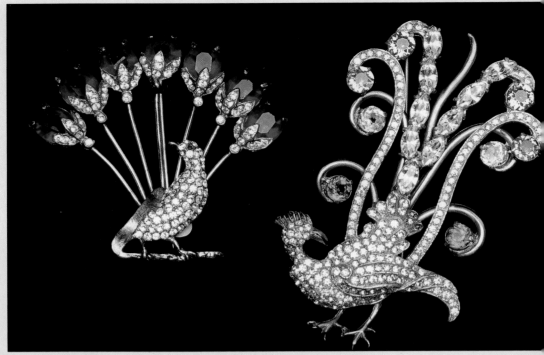

Two rhodium peacock brooches, from left: with clear rhinestones and red faceted glass, $210, and with clear, green, yellow, turquoise, and pink rhinestones, $195.

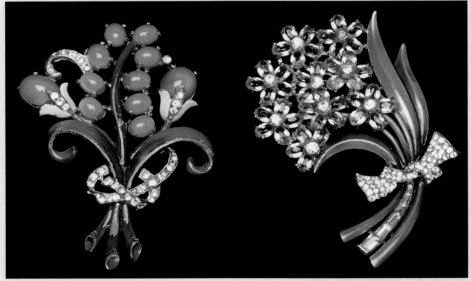

Floral brooches, from left: pot metal floral with clear rhinestones, pink cabochons, and enameling, $165, and Pennino with clear rhinestones, lavender faceted glass, and enameling, $345.

Pot metal brooches, clockwise from left: deer with clear, red, and green rhinestones, $85; horse with clear rhinestones, $95; and elephant with clear and red rhinestones and enameling, $125.

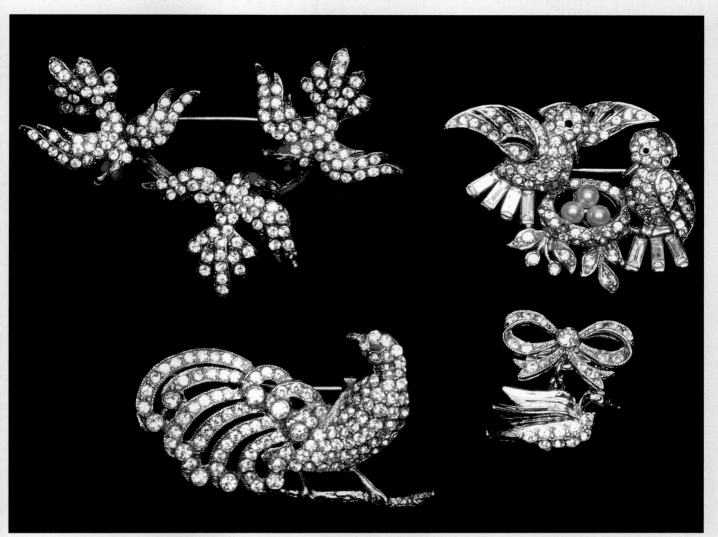

*Assorted bird brooches, clockwise from top left: pot metal with clear and red rhinestones, $145;
Boucher with clear rhinestones and faux pearls, $225; Ora with clear rhinestones, $65;
and pot metal with clear rhinestones, $155.*

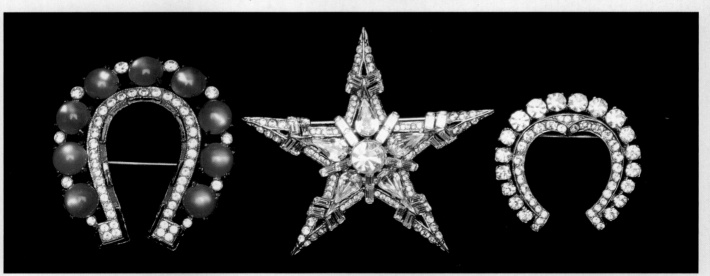

*More brooches, from left: pot metal horseshoe with clear rhinestones, blue cabochons, and enameling, $110;
Reinad star with clear rhinestones, $225; and Mazer sterling horseshoe with clear rhinestones, $185.*

Pot metal floral motif brooches, clockwise from bottom left: with clear rhinestones and enameling, $145; with clear rhinestones and enameling, $185; and trembler with clear rhinestones, pink cabochons, and enameling, $155.

A selection of rhodium floral brooches, left to right: with clear, pink, light blue, and green rhinestones, $160; with clear rhinestones and pink open-back rhinestones, $190; and with clear and light blue rhinestones, $185.

Coro Duette and matching earrings with clear rhinestones and enameling, $425.

Pot metal brooches, all with clear and blue rhinestones, clockwise from top left: Art Deco, $110; F.N. Co., $245; and floral, $88.

Pot metal bird brooches, all with clear rhinestones and enameling, priced left to right: $110, $98, and $68.

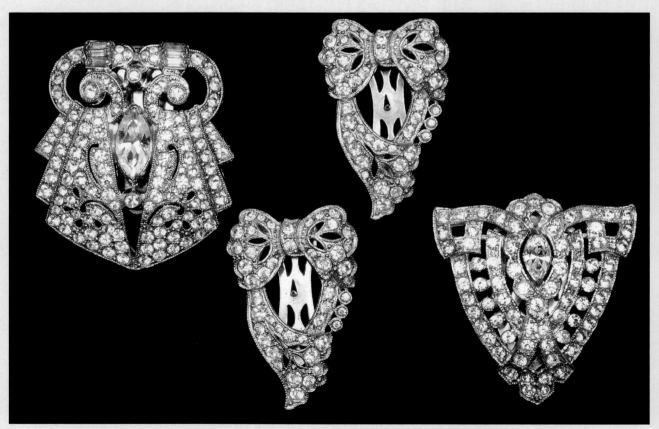

Pot metal and clear rhinestone dress clips, priced left to right: $125, $95 (pair), and, $95.

Pot metal and clear rhinestone pieces, clockwise from top left: brooch, $38; dress clip, $48; and brooch, $32.

Bow brooches, from left: pot metal with clear rhinestones, red cabochon, and enameling, $110, and rhodium with clear rhinestones and enameling, $245.

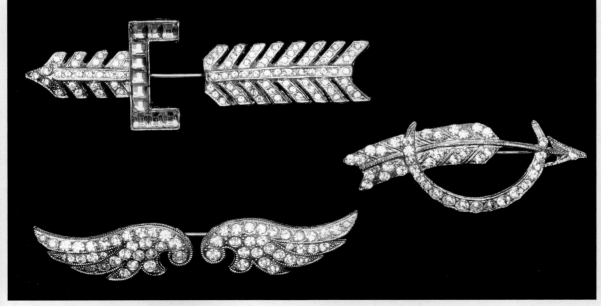

Pot metal and clear rhinestone brooches, priced clockwise from top left: $115, $88, and $68.

Pieces with clear and red rhinestones, from left: Corocraft sterling flower brooch, $225, and Jomaz earrings, $95.

Brooches, from left: rhodium with clear, red, green, and blue rhinestones, $265,
and pot metal with clear rhinestones, $140.

Matching sterling necklace, bracelet, and pin with clear rhinestones and blue faceted glass, $485.

Pot metal brooches, clockwise from top left: circus rider with clear and red rhinestones and enameling, $135;
Schiaparelli unicorn with clear and green rhinestones and enameling, $215;
and zebra with clear and red rhinestones and enameling, $165.

Pot metal dress clips, all with clear and blue rhinestones, priced from top: $110 (pair) and $72.

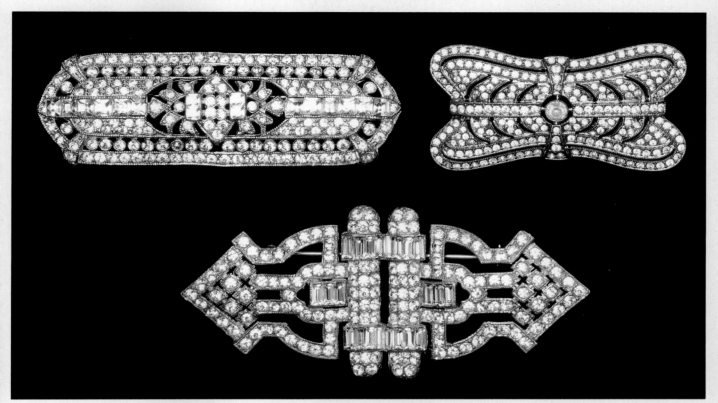

Clear rhinestone Art Deco brooches, clockwise from top left: pot metal, $165; rhodium, $155; and pot metal, $185.

Two rhodium brooches, both with clear rhinestones and faceted glass, from left: $225 and $295.

Floral motif brooches, left to right: pot metal with clear rhinestones, red cabochons, and enameling, $88; rhodium with clear rhinestones and enameling, $135; and pot metal with clear and red rhinestones, $105.

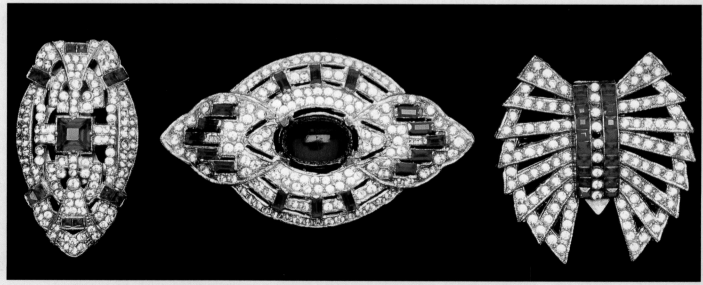

Pot metal pieces, all with clear and red rhinestones, left to right: dress clip, $135; Art Deco brooch, $135 (also has red cabochon); dress clip, $125.

Flower motif brooches, from left: Coro trembler with clear and lavender rhinestones and enameling, $165; Staret with clear rhinestones and faux pearl, $275; and pot metal trembler with clear rhinestones and glass beads, $95.

Patriotic brooches, clockwise from top left: pot metal flag with clear and red rhinestones and enameling, $165; three-dimensional rhodium eagle with clear rhinestones, $225; rhodium eagle with clear, red, and blue rhinestones, $88; and pot metal eagle with clear and blue rhinestones, $145.

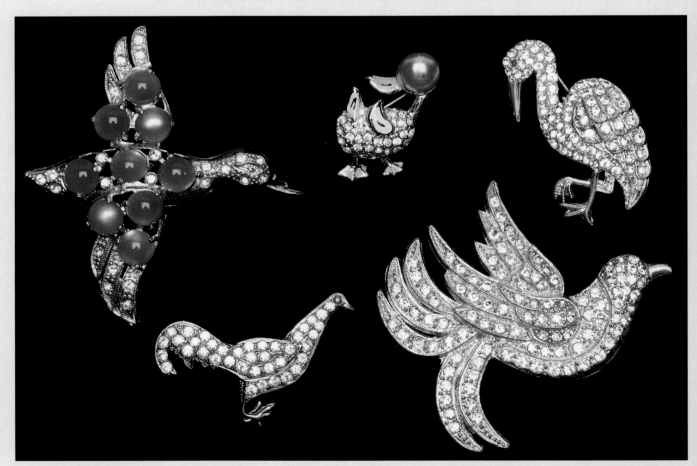

Various bird brooches, from top left: pot metal with clear rhinestones, blue cabochons, and enameling, $98; Coro duck with clear rhinestones, faux pearl, and enameling, $68; pot metal with clear and red rhinestones, $90; pot metal with clear rhinestones, $115; and rhodium with clear and red rhinestones, $85.

Four pot metal pieces covered in clear and green rhinestones, clockwise from top: Duette, $165; dress clip, $130; dress clip, $145; and dress clip, $135.

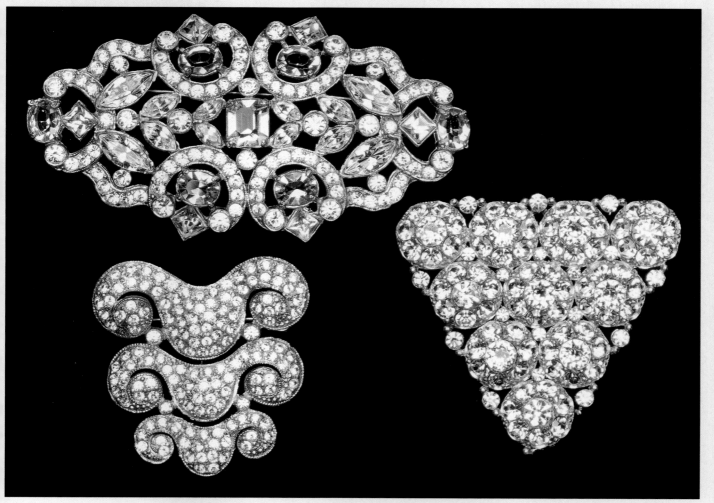

*Clear rhinestone brooches, clockwise from top left:
$195 (also with clear open-back rhinestones); Doctor Dress, $165; and Art Deco, $165.*

Three bird brooches, all of pot metal with clear rhinestones and enameling, clockwise from top: eagle, $295; owl on branch (also has green rhinestones), $135; and owl, $185.

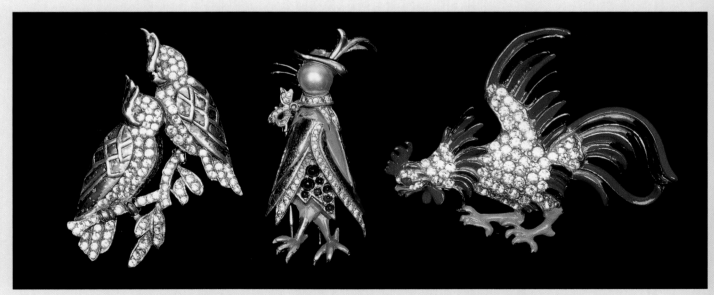

From left: Rhodium bird brooch with clear rhinestones and enameling, $195; rhodium bird fur clip with clear rhinestones, red and blue cabochons, faux pearl, and enameling, $165; and Staret rooster brooch with clear rhinestones and enameling, $265.

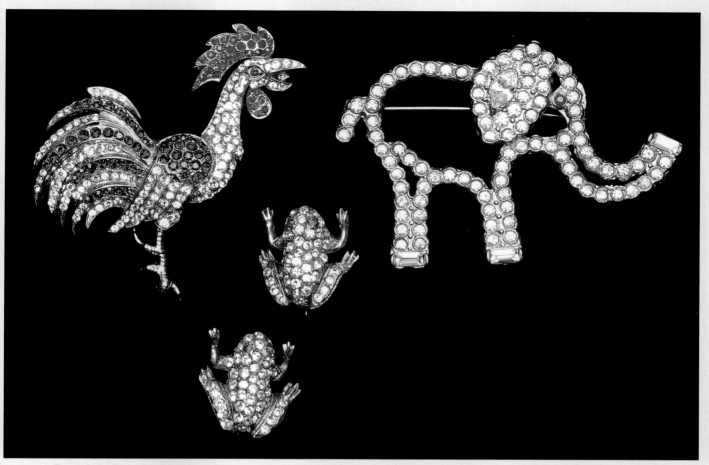

*From left: Rhodium rooster brooch with clear, red, and green rhinestones as well as enameling, $165;
two pot metal frog brooches with clear and green rhinestones, $90;
and pot metal elephant brooch with clear and red rhinestones, $98.*

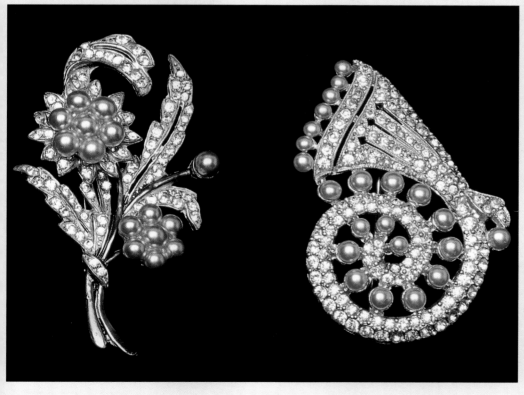

*Left: Rhodium floral brooch with clear rhinestones, faux pearls, and enameling, $185.
Right: Pot metal Art Deco brooch with clear rhinestones and faux pearls, $124.*

Three pot metal brooches with clear rhinestones, from top: $125, $120, and $85.

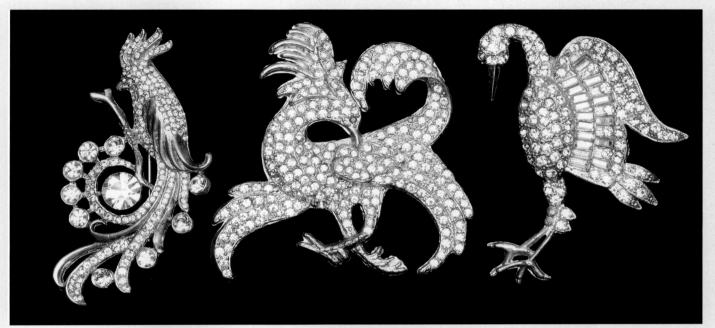

A trio of pot metal birds, left to right: brooch with clear and blue rhinestone, $155; brooch with clear and red rhinestones, $195; and pin with clear rhinestones, $145.

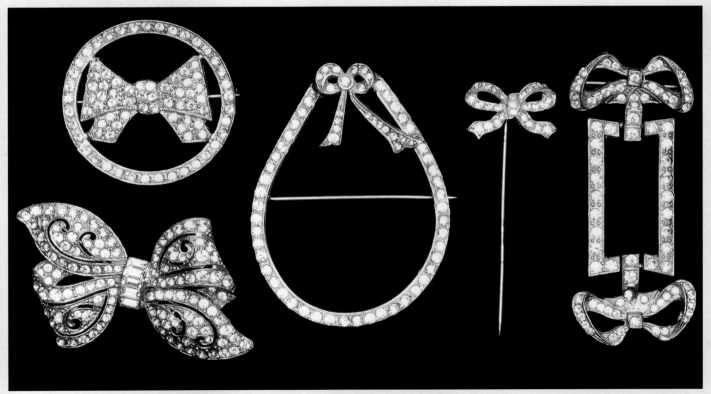

Several pot metal items, all with clear rhinestones, counterclockwise from top left: circular brooch with bow, $95; bow brooch, $125; oblong brooch with bow, $85; bow stickpin, $32; and double bow brooch, $90.

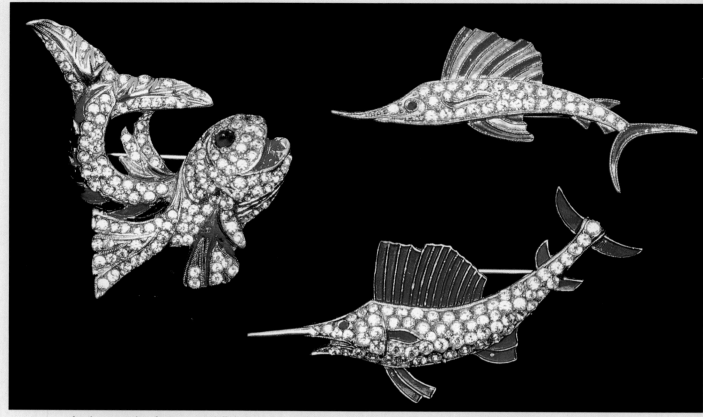

A nice catch of pot metal fish brooches, clockwise from left: with clear rhinestones, red cabochon, and enameling, $155; with clear and red rhinestones and enameling, $98; and another with clear and red rhinestones and enameling, $115.

Pot metal question mark brooch and matching earrings with clear rhinestones, $145.

Sterling pieces with marcasites, from left: brooch, $88, and dress clip, $98.

Trifari brooch and matching earrings with clear and red rhinestones, $285.

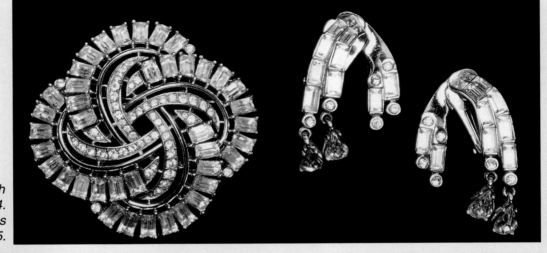

Left: Trifari brooch with clear rhinestones, $94.
Right: Rhodium earrings with clear rhinestones, $65.

Clear rhinestone pieces, from left: rhodium fur clip, $95; pot metal dress clip, $95; and pot metal dress clip, $98.

Two clear rhinestone pot metal bird brooches, from left: $185 and $135.

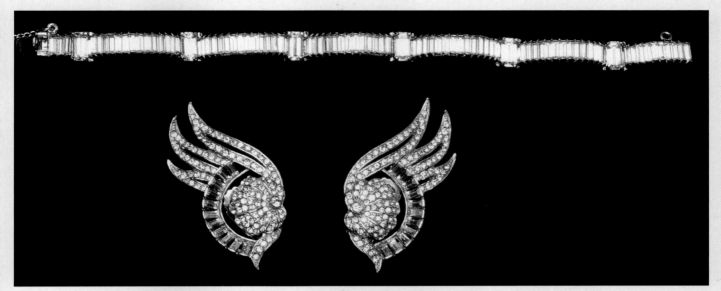

Clear rhinestone pieces, from top: rhodium bracelet, $195, and Wiesner earrings, $110.

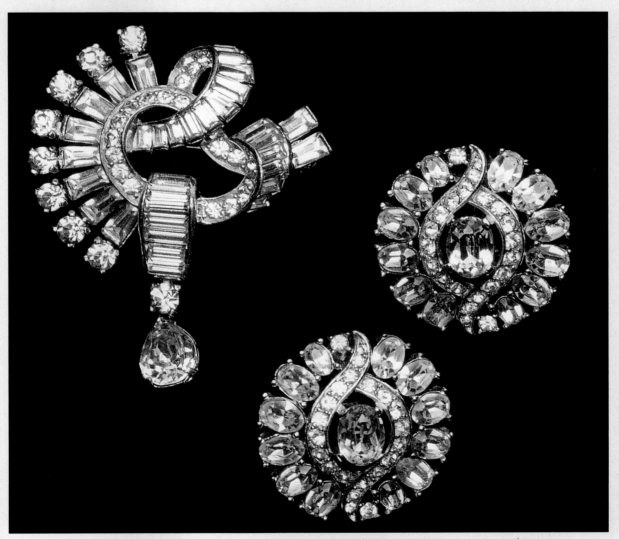

Clear rhinestone pieces, from left: Mazer brooch, $180, and Trifari earrings, $85.

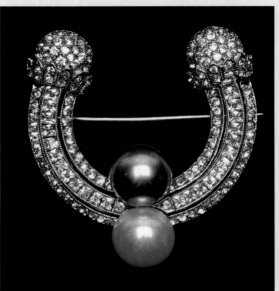

Sterling brooch with clear rhinestones and faux pearls, $225.

Top: Rhodium floral brooch with clear rhinestones as well as blue open-back rhinestones, $265.
Bottom: Sterling earrings with blue open-back rhinestones, $40.

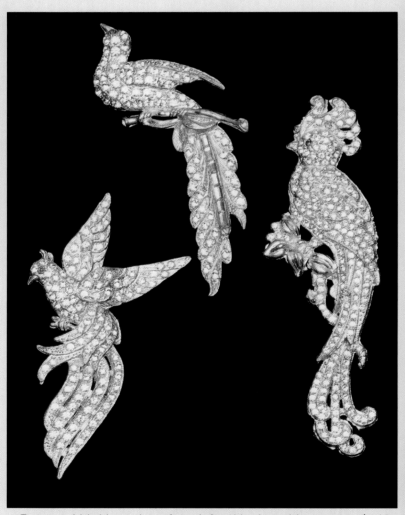

Pot metal bird brooches, from left: with clear rhinestones, $140; with clear and green rhinestones, $125; and with clear and blue rhinestones, $185.

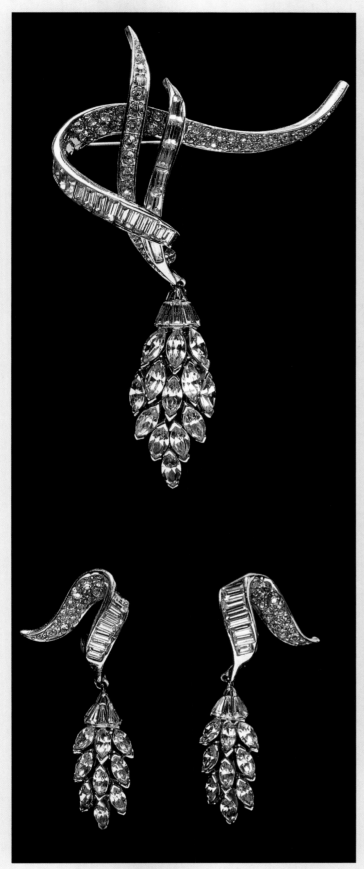

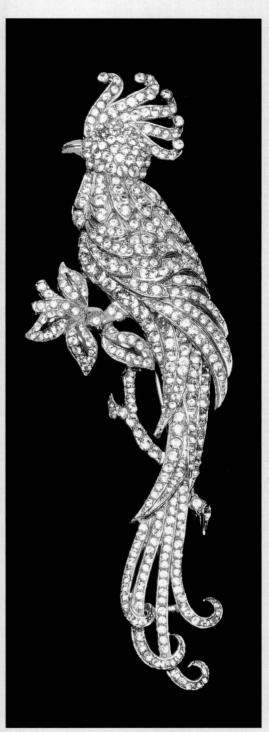

Corocraft bird brooch with clear rhinestones and enameling, $325.

Boucher brooch and matching earrings with clear rhinestones, $245.

Three clear rhinestone pot metal pieces, clockwise from top: circular brooch, $95; dress clip, $95; and dress clip, $110.

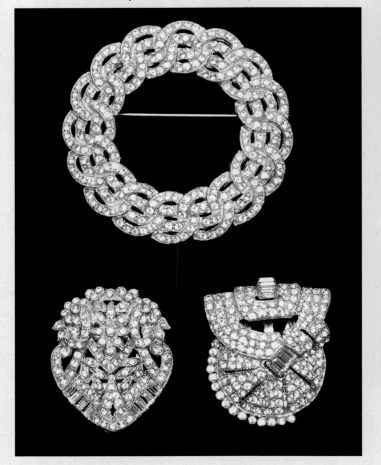

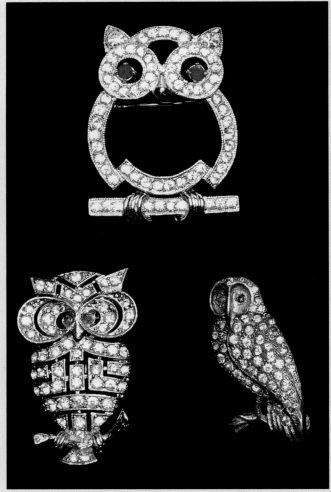

A trio of owl pins, clockwise from top: rhodium with clear and red rhinestones, $62; pot metal with clear and green rhinestones, $68; and pot metal with clear and green rhinestones, $55.

Top left and right: Reja brooch and matching earrings with clear and open-back rhinestones and faceted glass, $210. Bottom: Reja brooch with clear and open-back rhinestones, $145.

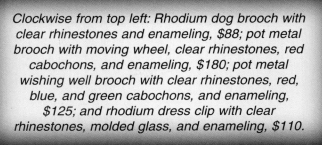

Clockwise from top left: Rhodium dog brooch with clear rhinestones and enameling, $88; pot metal brooch with moving wheel, clear rhinestones, red cabochons, and enameling, $180; pot metal wishing well brooch with clear rhinestones, red, blue, and green cabochons, and enameling, $125; and rhodium dress clip with clear rhinestones, molded glass, and enameling, $110.

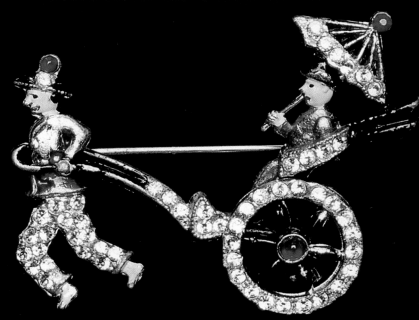

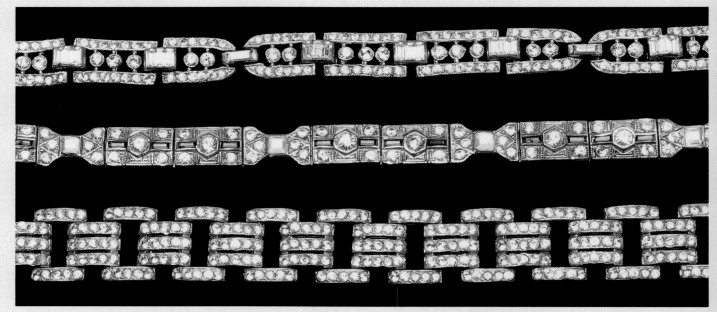

*Three bracelets, from top: pot metal with clear rhinestones, $155;
rhodium with clear and green rhinestones, $210; and pot metal with clear rhinestones, $225.*

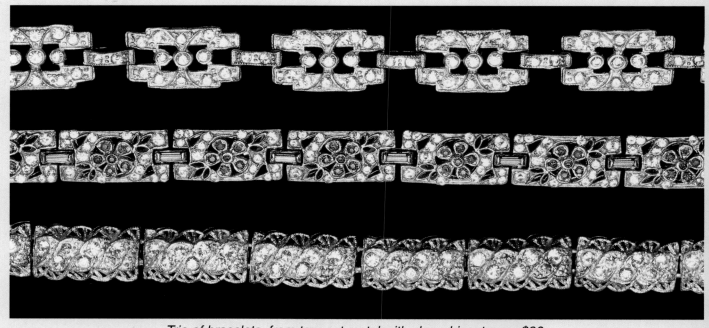

*Trio of bracelets, from top: pot metal with clear rhinestones, $96;
rhodium with clear and blue rhinestones, $195; and pot metal with clear rhinestones, $85.*

Top: Faux pearl bracelet with pot metal clasp and clear rhinestones, $155.
Bottom: Pot metal earrings with clear rhinestones and faux pearls, $45.

From left: Mazer flower basket brooch with clear rhinestones and molded glass, $245; rhodium leaf pin with clear rhinestones, $115; and sterling earrings with clear rhinestones and light blue faceted glass, $110.

*Reja matching
necklace, bracelet,
and earrings
with clear
and open-back
rhinestones, $265.*

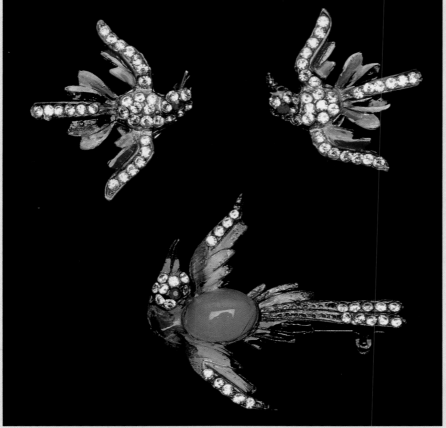

*Pot metal bird brooch and matching
earrings with clear and red rhinestones,
blue cabochon, and enameling, $165.*

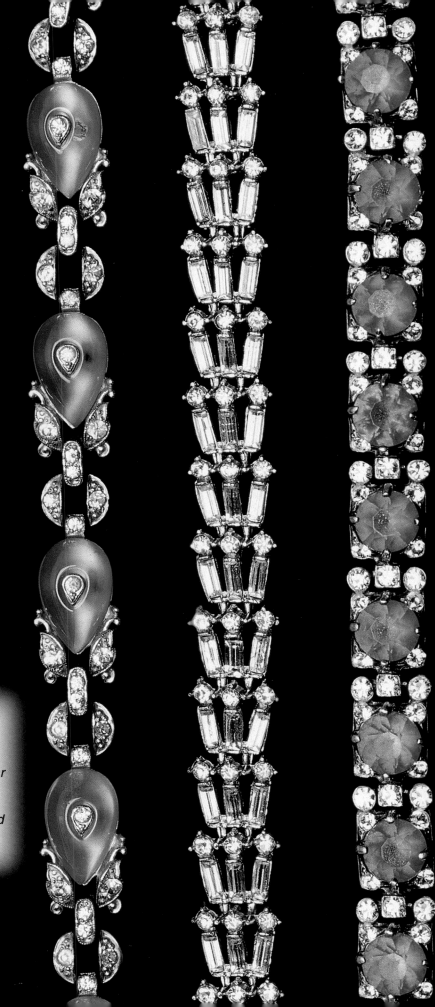

Bracelets, from left: Trifari with clear rhinestones and pink cabochons, $155; Trifari with clear rhinestones, $145; and sterling with clear rhinestones and blue faceted glass, $325.

Pot metal brooches, clockwise from top left: with clear and amethyst rhinestones, $185; with clear rhinestones, $82; and another with clear rhinestones, $92.

Pot metal floral motif brooches, from left: with clear rhinestones and enameling, $115; another with clear rhinestones and enameling, $195; and with green rhinestones and enameling, $98.

Clockwise from top left: Sterling ring with blue faceted glass, $95; sterling floral design brooch with clear and blue rhinestones, $155; rhodium Art Deco brooch with clear and blue rhinestones, blue faceted glass, and enameling, $185; and pot metal brooch with clear rhinestones and molded glass, $115.

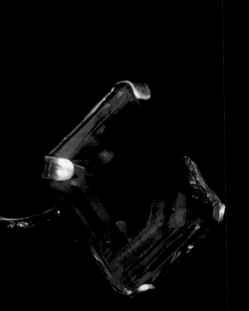

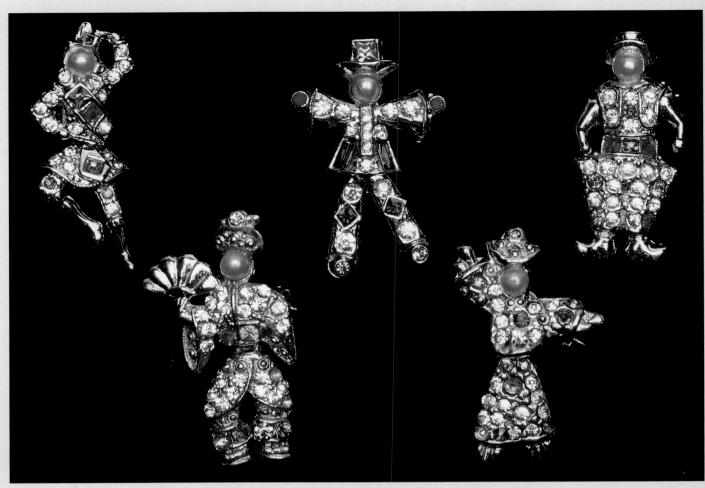

Scatter pins with rhinestones, $45 each.

Pot metal necklace and earrings (not a matching set), both with clear rhinestones, $98 and $110.

Pennino floral necklace with clear rhinestones, $210.

Rhodium floral necklace with clear rhinestones, $185.

Trifari necklace with clear and blue rhinestones, $225.

Three pairs of clear rhinestone earrings, left to right: Eisenberg, $110; pot metal, $85; and rhodium, $115.

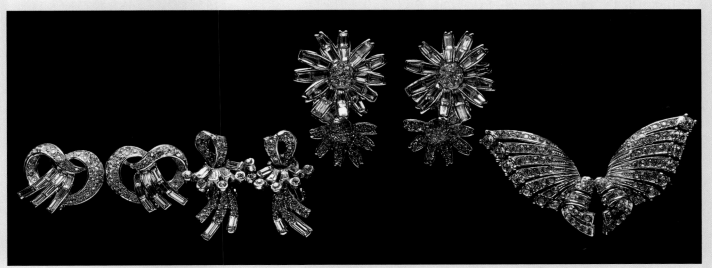

Four more pairs of clear rhinestone earrings, left to right: Trifari, $76;
Pell earrings, $65; and two Boucher sets, $125 and $110.

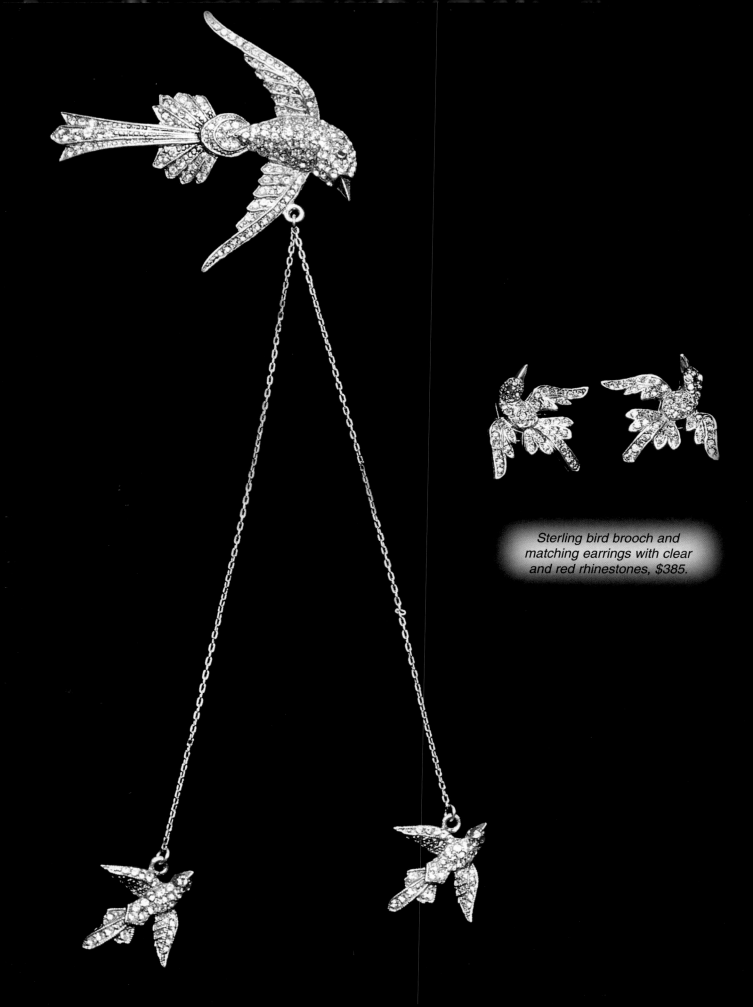

Sterling bird brooch and matching earrings with clear and red rhinestones, $385.

Pot metal dress clips, from left: with clear rhinestones and topaz, red, green, and light blue faceted glass, $145, and a pair with clear rhinestones and blue faceted glass, $145.

Three clear rhinestone pot metal brooches, clockwise from left: $165, $125, and $148.

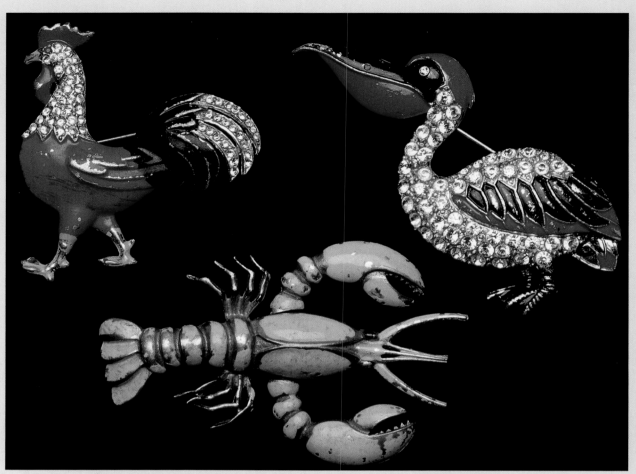

A trio of pot metal creatures, clockwise from top left: rooster brooch with clear and red rhinestones and enameling, $145; pelican brooch with clear rhinestones and enameling, $195; and enameled lobster pin with moveable claws, $125.

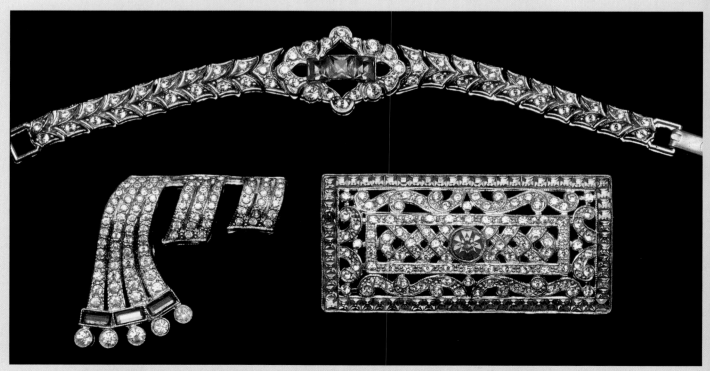

An ensemble of pot metal pieces, all with clear and blue rhinestones, priced clockwise from top: bracelet, $155; brooch, $185; and dress clip, $65.

*Pot metal pieces, from left: floral brooch with clear, red, blue, pink, amethyst, and green rhinestones, $195;
dress clip with clear, red, green, amethyst, blue, and pink rhinestones, $125;
and dress clip with blue, red, green, topaz, pink, and amethyst rhinestones, $80.*

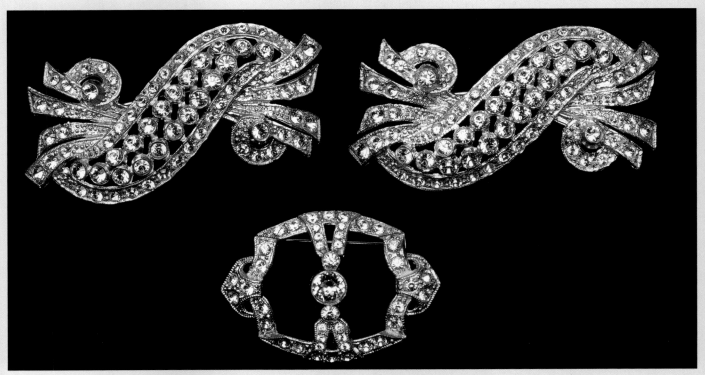

Brooches with clear rhinestones, from top: pair of Select, $125, and pot metal, $55.

Pot metal pieces, clockwise from top left: earrings with clear rhinestones and molded glass, $135; flower dress clip with clear and amethyst rhinestones, $62; and pendant with clear rhinestones and amethyst glass beads, $145.

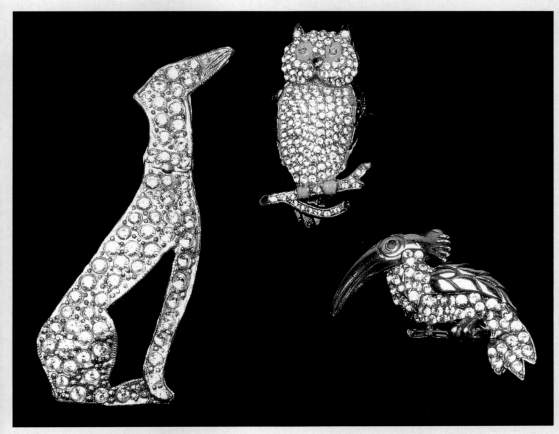

Brooches, left to right: pot metal dog with clear rhinestones, $75; pot metal owl with clear and topaz rhinestones and enameling, $155; and rhodium toucan with clear and green rhinestones, $110.

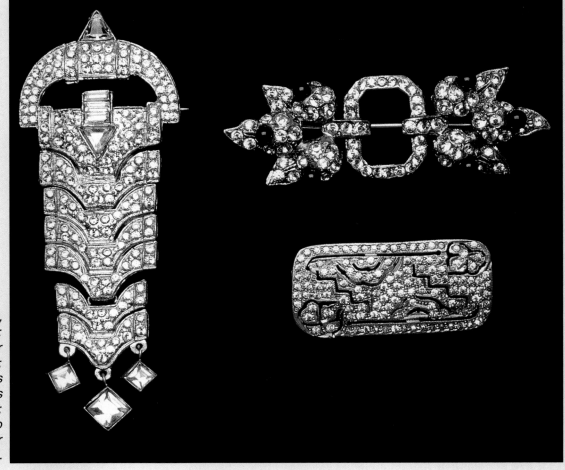

Pot metal brooches, clockwise from left: Art Deco with clear rhinestones, $225; with clear rhinestones and black glass beads, $125; and Art Deco design with clear rhinestones, $65.

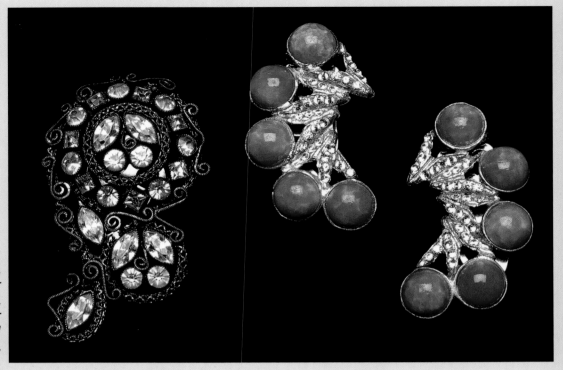

Pot metal dress clips, from left: with clear rhinestones, $78, and a pair with clear rhinestones and cabochons, $90.

Clockwise from top left: Rhodium floral basket brooch with clear, pink, topaz, and green rhinestones, $145; pot metal bow brooch with clear rhinestones, $145; pot metal heart fur clip with clear rhinestones, $135; and pot metal bow brooch with clear rhinestones, $65.

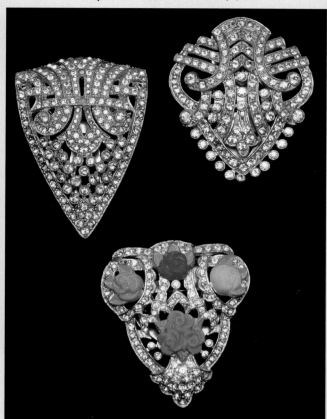

Dress clips, clockwise from left:
rhodium Art Deco with clear rhinestones, $95;
pot metal Art Deco with clear rhinestones, $95;
and pot metal with flowers, $98.

Brooches, top to bottom: pot metal with clear rhinestones
and faceted glass, $85; rhodium flower trembler with
clear and red rhinestones, $165; and pot metal
flower trembler with clear rhinestones, $135.

Clockwise from top: Rhodium bracelet with clear rhinestones, $165;
pot metal earrings with clear rhinestones, $38; and sterling crown brooch with clear rhinestones, $58.

Three crown brooches, from top: Trifari with clear, red, blue, and green rhinestones, $155; Corocraft three-dimensional with clear rhinestones, $185; and Corocraft sterling with clear rhinestones, $145.

A trio of pot metal brooches, left to right: floral basket with clear and blue open-back rhinestones, $85; bird with clear and blue rhinestones, $30; and floral design with blue rhinestones, $65.

Three more pot metal pieces, from left: leaf brooch with blue rhinestones, $28; dress clip with clear and blue rhinestones, $85; and brooch with clear and blue rhinestones, $88.

Pot metal pieces with clear and blue rhinestones, from top: brooch, $165, and pair of dress clips, $95.

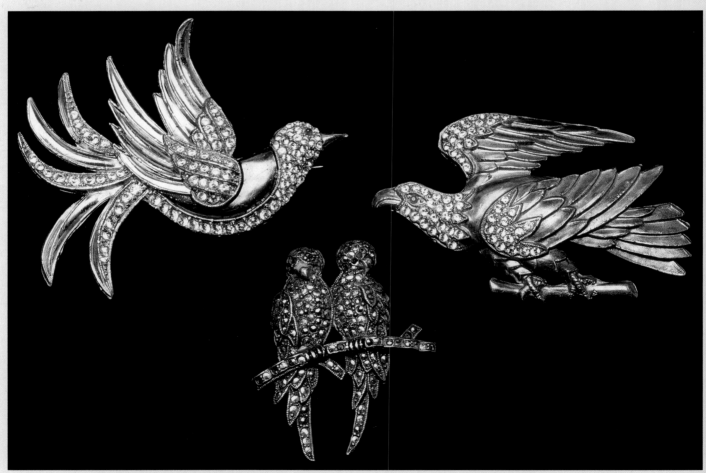

Bird brooches, left to right: rhodium with clear and pink rhinestones and enameling, $125; pot metal with marcasites, $95; and pot metal with clear and red rhinestones, $85.

Clockwise from left: Pot metal floral brooch with clear rhinestones and enameling, $145; rhodium flower dress clip with clear and green rhinestones and enameling, $65; and pot metal pear fur clip with amethyst, topaz, red, blue, and green rhinestones and enameling, $65.

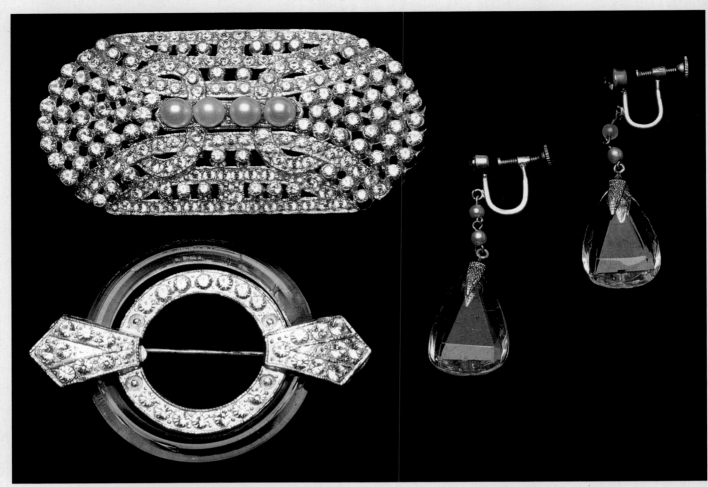

Clockwise from top left: Pot metal brooch with clear rhinestones and faux pearls, $145; sterling earrings with clear rhinestones, faux pearls, and faceted glass, $85; and pot metal Art Deco brooch with clear rhinestones and glass, $110.

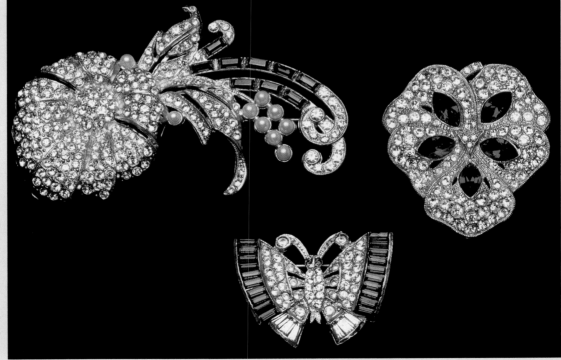

Pot metal pieces, clockwise from top left: flower brooch with clear and green rhinestones and faux pearls, $185; dress clip with clear and green rhinestones, $85; and butterfly brooch with clear and green rhinestones, $110.

*Clockwise from top left:
Rhodium court jester brooch
with green, blue, red, and
pink rhinestones, $195;
pot metal king fur clip with clear,
topaz, green, and amethyst
rhinestones, $90; and pot metal
woman's face brooch with
citrine rhinestones, $85.*

A selection of pot metal butterflies, clockwise from top left: brooch with clear and blue rhinestones, $285; brooch with clear and red rhinestones, $110; brooch with clear and blue rhinestones, $65; and clip with clear rhinestones, $45.

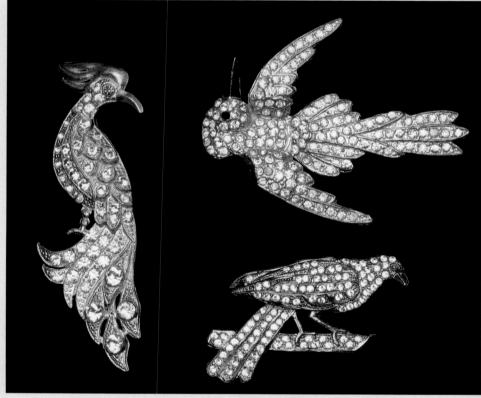

Pot metal bird brooches, clockwise from left: with clear rhinestones, $135; with clear rhinestones, $145; and with clear and red rhinestones, $85.

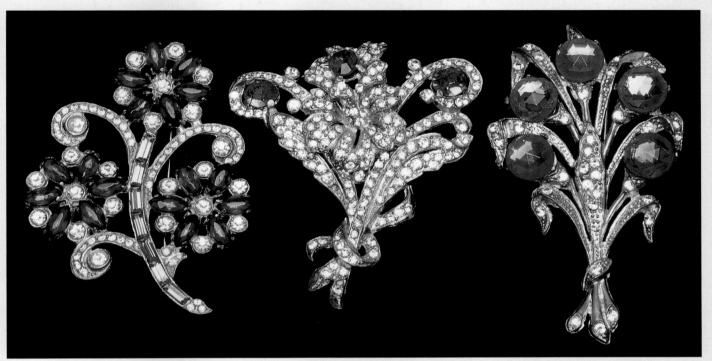

Three pot metal brooches, all with clear and blue rhinestones, priced left to right: $145, $185, and $95.

Pot metal brooches, clockwise from top left: anchor with clear rhinestones, $32;
woman's face with clear, red, and green rhinestones, $110; and wishbone with clear rhinestones, $16.

*Clockwise from left:
Pot metal bangle with
clear and green rhinestones, $165;
pot metal dress clip with
clear rhinestones and
green glass cabochon, $85;
and sterling earrings with
clear and green rhinestones, $80.*

*Clear rhinestone
pieces, clockwise
from top left: Allco
rhodium bangle, $165;
pot metal floral
necklace, $125;
and pot metal ring, $80.*

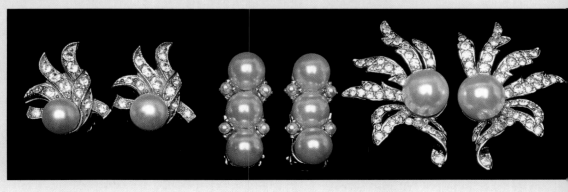

*Three pairs of
earrings, from left:
rhodium with
clear rhinestones
and faux pearls, $45;
rhodium with
faux pearls, $40;
and sterling with
clear rhinestones and
faux pearls, $74.*

Pot metal pieces, from top:
grape design dress clip with
opalescent cabochons and enameling,
$85, and berry brooch with clear
rhinestones and glass beads, $135.

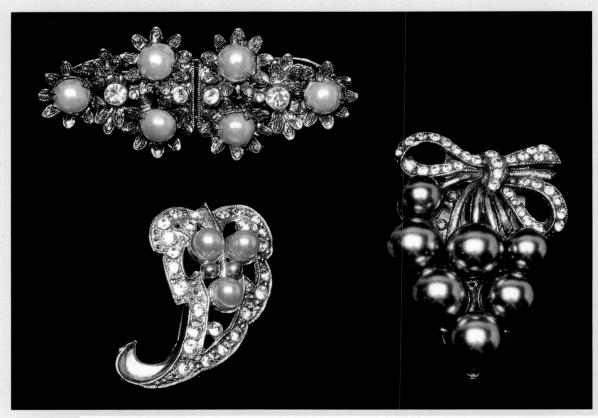

Pot metal pieces, all with clear rhinestones and faux pearls, clockwise from top left: Duette, $98; dress clip, $74; and brooch, $48.

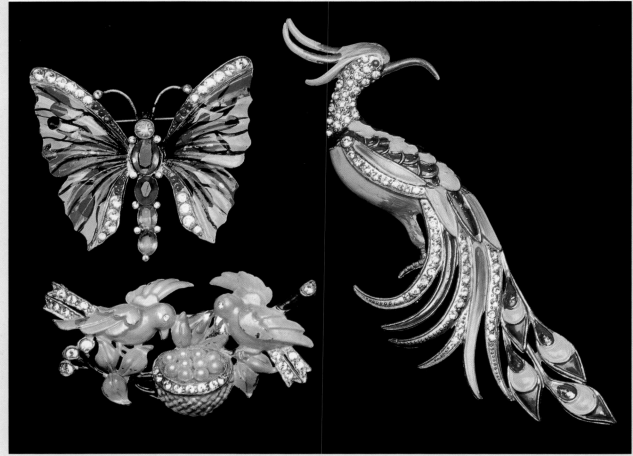

Pot metal brooches, clockwise from top left: butterfly with clear, red, blue, and topaz rhinestones and enameling, $145; bird with clear rhinestones and enameling, $185; and bird with clear rhinestones, faux pearls, and enameling, $125.

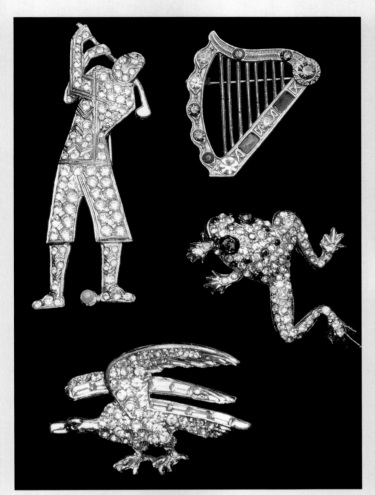

Brooches, from left: Jomaz with clear rhinestones, $185, and Ledo with clear rhinestones and faux pearl, $60.

Brooches, clockwise from top left: base metal golfer with clear rhinestones and faux pearl, $65; pot metal harp with red, green, topaz, blue, and amethyst rhinestones, $35; rhodium frog with clear rhinestones, green cabochons, and enameling, $65; and rhodium eagle with clear and green rhinestones, $65.

From left: Staret brooch with clear rhinestones, $325; pot metal dress clip with open-back rhinestones, $155; and pot metal dress clip with clear rhinestones, $165.

Trifari floral fur clip with clear rhinestones and enameling, $325.

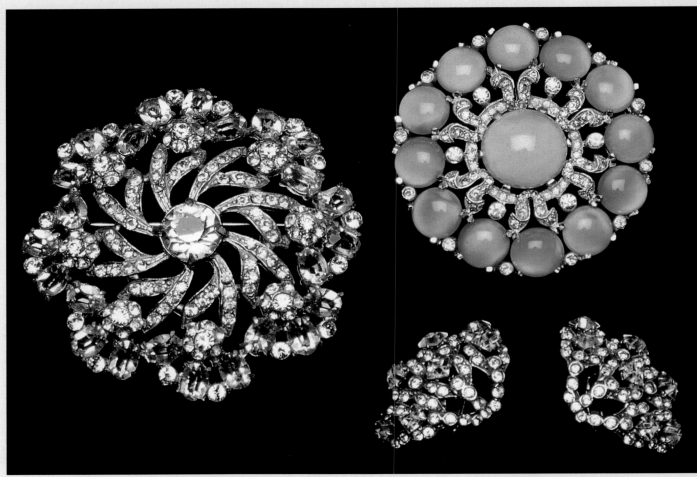

Clockwise from left: Rhodium brooch with clear rhinestones and open-back rhinestones, $95;
rhodium brooch with clear rhinestones and blue cabochons, $125; sterling earrings with clear rhinestones, $95.

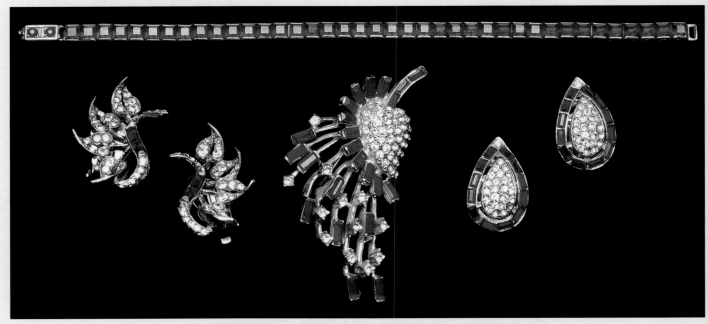

Top: Sterling bracelet with red rhinestones, $135.
On bottom, rhodium pieces, all with clear and red rhinestones, left to right:
earrings, $65; brooch, $85; pair of earrings, $60.

Floral brooches, from left: Staret with clear rhinestones and white enameling, $390, and pot metal with clear rhinestones and white and black enameling, $45.

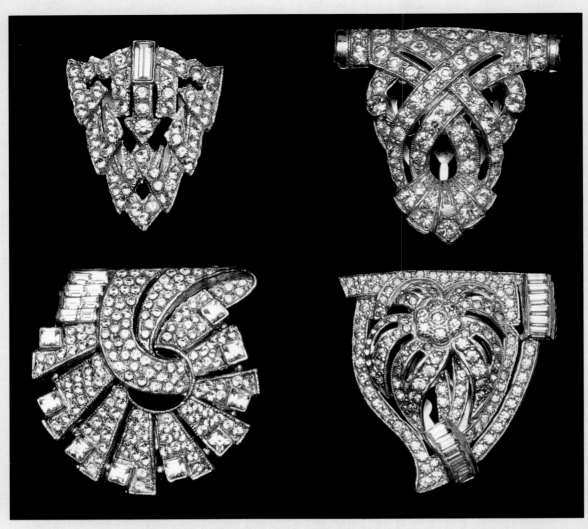

Pot metal dress clips, all with clear rhinestones, priced clockwise from top left: $45, $85 (also has blue glass), $90, and $110.

Clockwise from top left: Pot metal bow brooch with clear rhinestones and enameling, $98; pot metal bow brooch with clear rhinestones, faceted glass, and enameling, $65; rhodium earrings with clear rhinestones and enameling, $85.

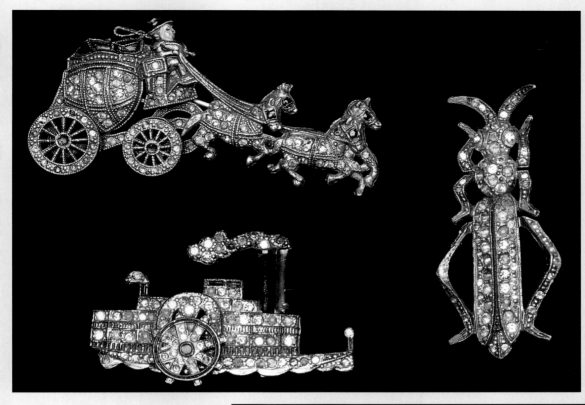

Pot metal brooches, clockwise from top left: horse and carriage with pink, blue, green, topaz, and amethyst rhinestones, $95; bug with clear, topaz, green, pink, and blue rhinestones, $65; and steamboat with clear, blue, topaz, green, pink, and amethyst rhinestones, $95.

Two pieces with clear rhinestones and enameling, from left: Trifari fur clip, $165, and pot metal floral brooch, $95.

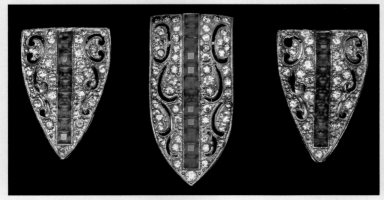

Three Art Deco dress clips with clear and red rhinestones, $195.

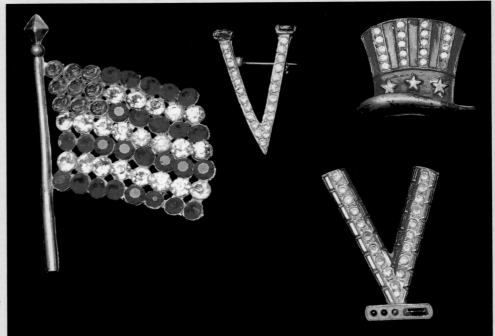

Four patriotic pot metal brooches, clockwise from left: flag with clear, red, and blue rhinestones, $145; "V" with clear, red, and blue rhinestones, $65; Uncle Sam hat with clear rhinestones and red and blue enameling, $95; and "V" with clear rhinestones as well as red and blue enameling, $60.

Floral brooches, from left Staret with clear rhinestones, $195; pot metal with clear and pink rhinestones, $125; and rhodium with clear rhinestones, $90.

Identical pot metal lizard brooches with clear rhinestones and enameling, $175 each.

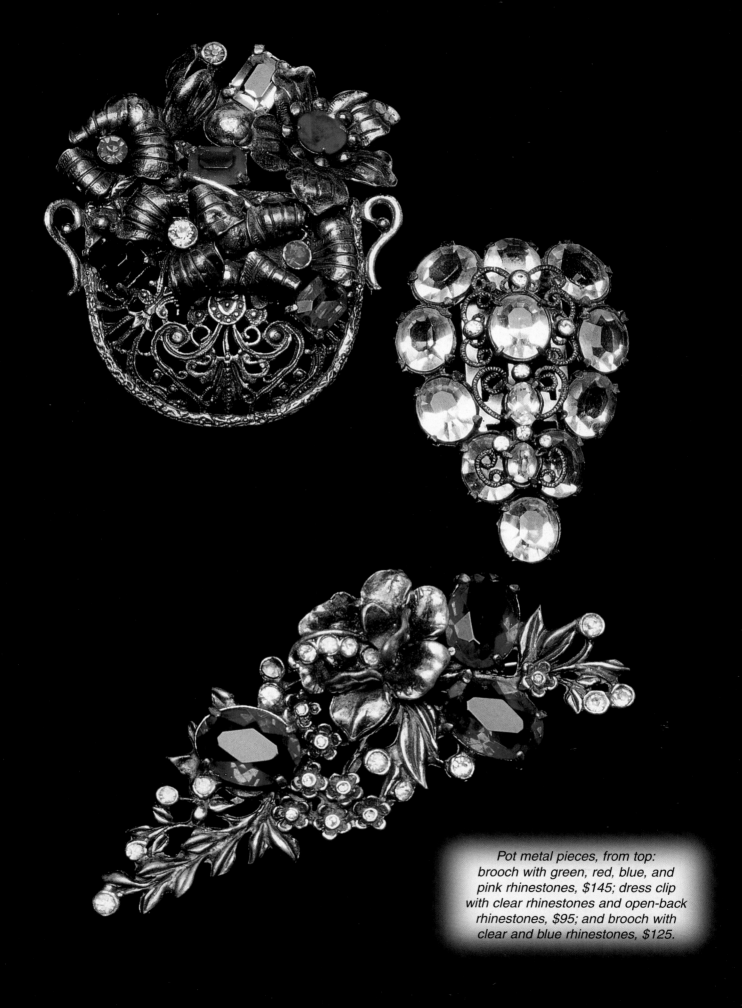

Pot metal pieces, from top: brooch with green, red, blue, and pink rhinestones, $145; dress clip with clear rhinestones and open-back rhinestones, $95; and brooch with clear and blue rhinestones, $125.

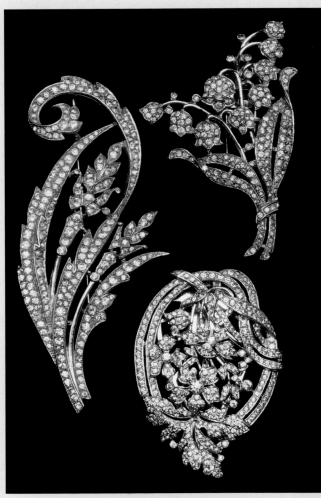

A trio of clear rhinestone Trifari, clockwise from left: floral brooch, $185; floral fur clip, $175; and dress clip, $135.

From top: Pot metal bow brooch with clear open-back rhinestones and blue cabochons, $265; pot metal brooch with clear rhinestones, $90; and rhodium dress clip with clear rhinestones, $195.

Eisenberg eagle brooch with clear rhinestones and enameling, $650.

*Pot metal pieces, from left: dress clip with amethyst rhinestones, $95,
and flower bouquet brooch with green rhinestones and molded glass leaves, $65.*

*Corocraft sterling jelly belly fish brooch
with clear and pink rhinestones and enameling, $495.*

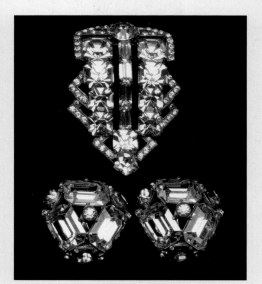

*Top: Eisenberg Original brooch
with clear rhinestones, $395.
Bottom: Pair of pot metal dress clips
with clear rhinestones, $85.*

Clockwise from top left: Rhodium sword brooch with green, amethyst, red, blue, and topaz rhinestones, $65; pot metal floral bouquet brooch with light blue rhinestones and enameling, $145; pot metal cat fur clip with lavender rhinestone and faceted blue glass belly, $45.

Clear rhinestone pieces, clockwise from top left: Eisenberg Original brooch, $450; pot metal dress clip, $75; and Eisenberg Original sterling fur clip, $395.

An assortment of floral brooches, from left: pot metal basket with clear rhinestones and green, blue, yellow, and burgundy cabochons, $58; Leo Glass arrangement with clear, green, blue, pink, topaz, and amethyst rhinestones, $165; and pot metal basket with light blue rhinestones and faux turquoise cabochons, $62.

Brooches, from left: Jomaz leaf with clear rhinestones and blue open-back rhinestones, $95; Trifari with clear rhinestones, $45; and Boucher bow with clear rhinestones, $95.

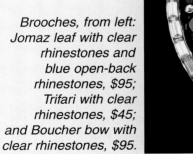

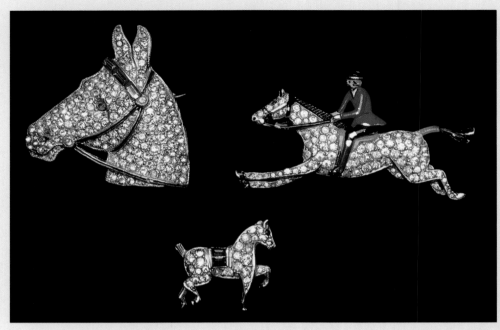

Horse motif pieces, clockwise from top left: pot metal head brooch with clear, blue, and green rhinestones, $110; Trifari horse and jockey brooch with clear rhinestones and enameling, $125; and Trifari pin with clear and blue rhinestones, $45.

Clockwise from top left: Coro Duette with clear rhinestones, $345; pot metal Duette with clear and blue rhinestones, $125; and rhodium Clipmate with clear rhinestones, $155.

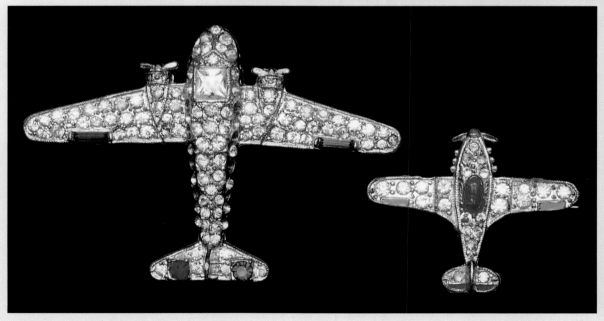

Pot metal airplane brooches, from left: with clear, red, and green rhinestones, $90, and with clear rhinestones and enameling, $45.

An assortment of ever-popular floral design items, from left: rhodium enameled brooch with marcasites, $145; Coro fur clip with clear and amethyst rhinestones and enameling, $85; sterling enameled brooch with marcasites, $165; and rhodium brooch with clear rhinestones, glass beads, and enameling, $245.

Bow brooches, clockwise from top left: Eisenberg Original with clear rhinestones, $385; pot metal with clear rhinestones, $195; Eisenberg Original with clear rhinestones and faceted glass, $345.

Staret brooch with clear rhinestones and green open-back rhinestones, $745.

Clear rhinestone pieces, clockwise from left: rhodium bracelet, $245; Trifari fur clip, $225; and pot metal earrings, $42.

Trifari fur clips with clear rhinestones and enameling, from left $325 (trembler also with faux pearl), $195, and $155.

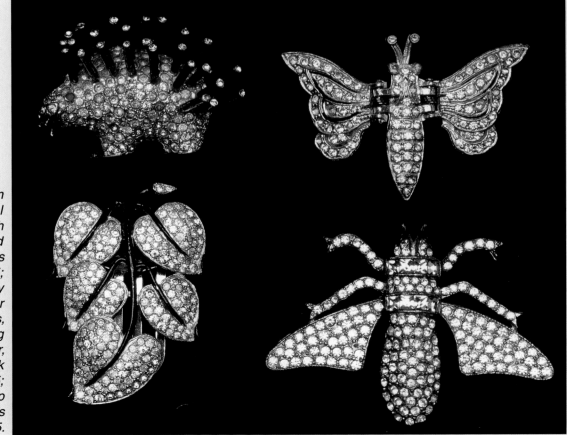

Clockwise from top left: Pot metal porcupine brooch with clear and red rhinestones and enameling, $145; pot metal butterfly brooch with clear and pink rhinestones, $85; Reinad bug brooch with clear, blue, and pink rhinestones, $325; and Trifari dress clip with clear rhinestones and enameling, $165.

Brooches, with clear rhinestones, clockwise from top left: Coro enameled flamingo, $295; Jomaz enameled mallard, $145; and pot metal enameled grasshopper, $95.

Pot metal floral brooches, from left: with clear and green rhinestones, $165; with clear rhinestones, $110; and another with clear rhinestones, $90.

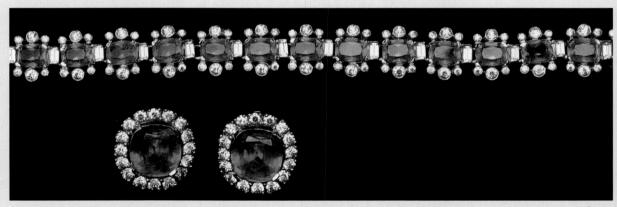

Jomaz bracelet and matching earrings with clear rhinestones and green open-back rhinestones, $195.

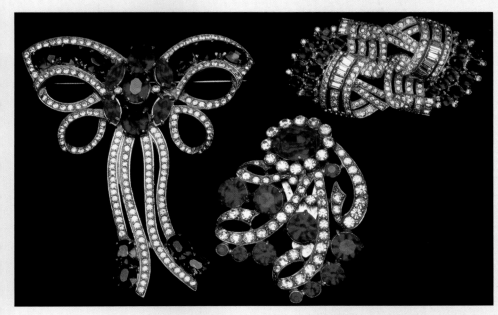

From left: Eisenberg Original bow brooch with clear, red, and amethyst rhinestones, $545; Staret dress clip with clear and red rhinestones, $245; and rhodium brooch with clear and red rhinestones, $165.

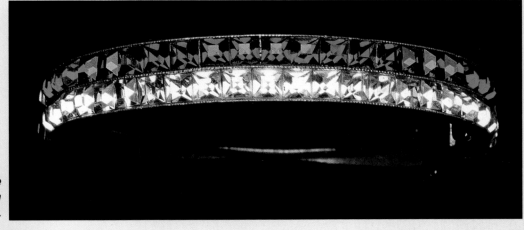

Pot metal bangle with clear and green rhinestones, $195.

Alfred Philippe necklace with clear and red rhinestones, $625.

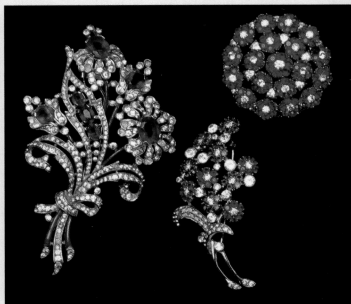

Clockwise from left: Trifari fur clip with red and clear rhinestones and enameling, $345; Trifari brooch with clear and red rhinestones, $110; and Jomaz floral brooch with clear, red, and blue rhinestones, $85.

Pot metal pieces, from top: brooch with clear rhinestones, $65; Art Deco brooch with clear rhinestones, $145; and pendant with faceted glass on faceted glass bead necklace, $85.

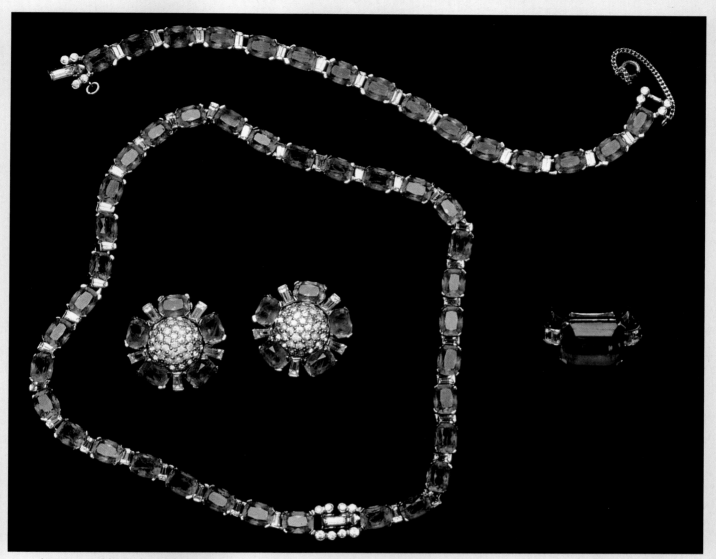

Jomaz necklace, bracelet, earrings, and ring with clear rhinestones and green open-back rhinestones, $245.

Left to right: Sterling pendant with clear and green rhinestones, $145; AJ pot metal bug brooch with clear rhinestones and green faceted glass, $155; and pot metal dress clip with clear and green rhinestones, $60.

Pot metal brooches, from left: bird with blue rhinestones and enameling, $85; floral with clear rhinestones and enameling, $145; and pear with clear rhinestones and enameling, $110.

Three bow designs, clockwise from top: pot metal brooch with clear rhinestones, $225; pot metal dress clip, $65; and sterling brooch with clear rhinestones, $365.

Pot metal pieces, clockwise from top left: brooch with clear and red rhinestones, $98; pair of martini glass brooches, $65; and dress clip with clear and red rhinestones, $110.

Pot metal brooches, from left: floral with clear rhinestones, faux pearl, and enameling, $72, and bow with clear rhinestones, glass cabochon, and enameling, $110.

Two pot metal flower basket brooches, from left: with clear rhinestones and green cabochons, $80, and with clear rhinestones and pink cabochons, $95.

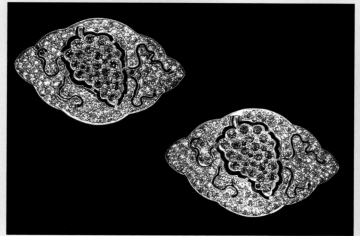

Pair of sterling grape design buckles with clear and amethyst rhinestones, $85.

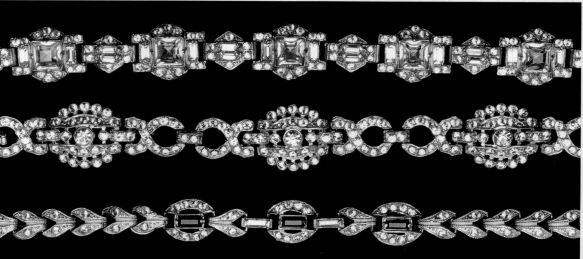

Three clear rhinestone pot metal bracelets, priced from top: $165, $185, and $110 (also has black rhinestones).

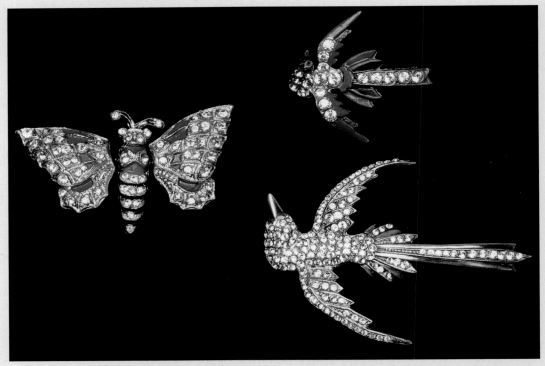

Assorted brooches, clockwise from left: pot metal butterfly brooch with moveable wings, clear rhinestones, and enameling, $145; pot metal bird brooch with clear rhinestones and enameling, $72; and sterling bird brooch with clear rhinestones, $165.

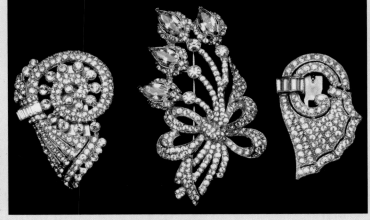

Clear rhinestone pieces, left to right: pot metal dress clip, $165; rhodium floral brooch, $185; and pot metal dress clip, $98.

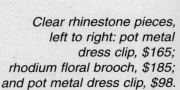

Two pot metal fish motif brooches, both with clear and blue rhinestones, priced from left: $98 and $110 (also has enameling).

Three filigree pendants, from top: with clear rhinestones, $165; with blue and clear rhinestones, $110; and with clear and blue rhinestones, $195.

Clear rhinestone pieces, from left: Trifari earrings, $95; rhodium brooch, $90; and another rhodium brooch, $125.

Three sets of earrings, all with clear rhinestones, clockwise from top left: sterling, $65; pot metal, $38; and pot metal, $35.

Two pairs pot metal earrings with clear rhinestones, both $125.

Assortment of earrings, from left: pot metal with clear, topaz, blue, pink, and amethyst rhinestones, $74; sterling with pink rhinestones, $125; and pot metal with blue rhinestones, $42.

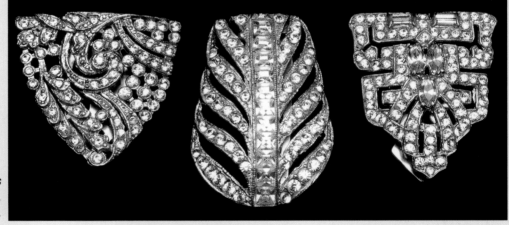

Three pot metal dress clips with clear rhinestones, from left: $85, $95, and $95.

Pot metal and rhinestone buttons, $22 each.

Pot metal dress clip with clear rhinestones, $165.

Pot metal necklace with clear rhinestones, $195.

Pot metal with clear rhinestones, from top: bracelet, $195, and brooch, $85.

Pair of pot metal Art Deco dress clips with clear rhinestones, $215.

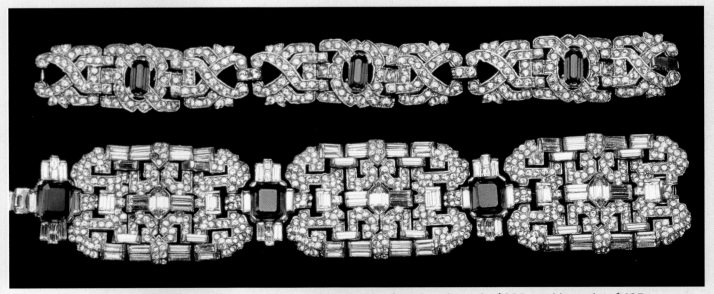

Rhodium pieces with clear and green rhinestones, from top: brooch, $225, and bracelet, $495.

Clockwise from left: Pot metal and clear rhinestone clasp on faux pearl double-strand necklace, $125; pot metal and clear rhinestone clasp on triple-strand faux pearl bracelet, $65; and pot metal dress clip with clear rhinestones and faux pearls, $55.

Pot metal and clear rhinestone items, clockwise from top left: pendant, $65; floral brooch, $65; and bar pin, $42.

Pot metal and clear rhinestone pieces, from left: bird brooch, $195, and dress clip, $125.

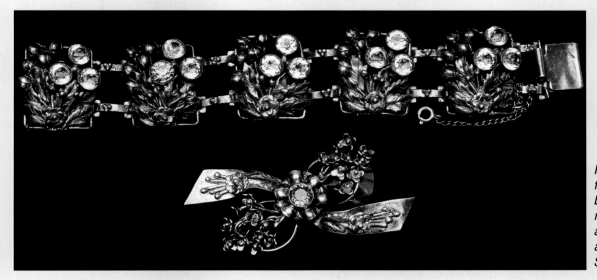

Hobe sterling pieces, from top: bracelet with blue open-back rhinestones, $325, and brooch with amethyst rhinestone, $190.

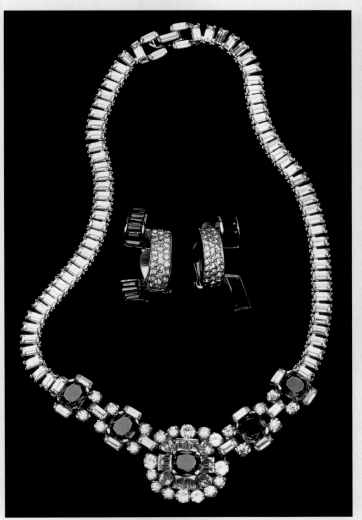

Jomaz necklace and matching earrings with clear and blue rhinestones, $295.

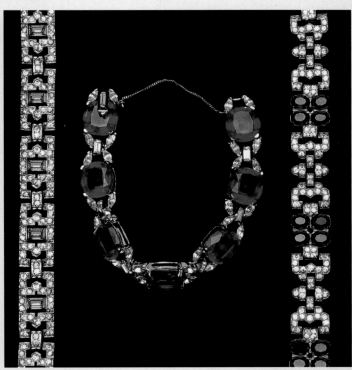

A variety of bracelets, from left: TKF with clear and blue rhinestones, $175; rhodium with clear rhinestones and pink open-back rhinestones, $245; and rhodium with clear rhinestones and blue open-back rhinestones, $225.

*Rhodium necklace
with clear rhinestones, $195.*

Rhodium brooch with clear and red rhinestones, $225.

Two rhodium pendants, from top: with clear rhinestones, $225, and with clear rhinestones and red open-back rhinestone, $245.

Pot metal brooch with clear rhinestones, $195.

Pot metal earrings with clear rhinestones, $125.

Pot metal and blue rhinestone assortment, clockwise from top left: dress clip, $65; brooch, $42; and earrings, $42.

Ensemble of pot metal pieces, all with clear and blue rhinestones, clockwise from top: bracelet, $110; earrings, $42; and brooch, $65.

A selection of pot metal brooches, clockwise from top left: bird with clear rhinestones, amethyst open-back rhinestones, and enameling, $125; lizard with clear rhinestones, $38; butterfly with red, topaz, green, amethyst, and blue rhinestones, $62; and butterfly with clear and pink rhinestones, $42.

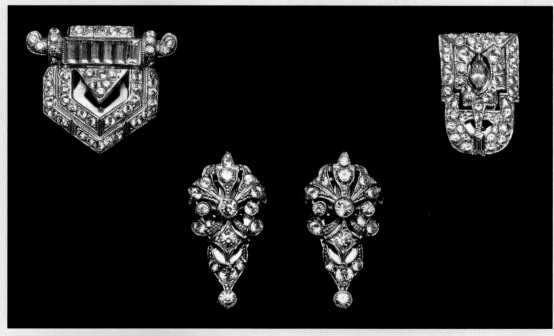

Dress clips with clear rhinestones, clockwise from top left: rhodium, $75; pot metal, $42; and a pair of pot metal, $78.

Pair of pot metal dress clips, $85.

*Two sterling pieces, from top: bracelet with clear rhinestones and green open-back rhinestones, $195,
and ring with clear rhinestones and faceted glass, $125.*

*Pot metal brooches
with clear rhinestones,
from left: leaf, $85,
and bow, $110.*

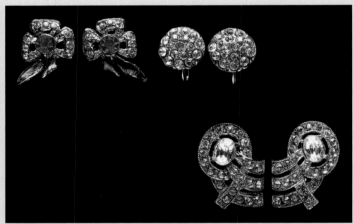

*Three pairs pot metal earrings, clockwise from top left:
with clear and pink rhinestones, $28;
with clear rhinestones, $32;
and another set with clear rhinestones, $45.*

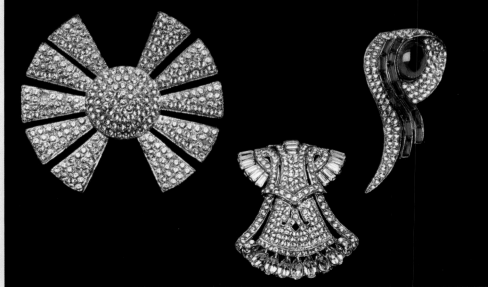

*Pot metal and clear rhinestone
pieces, left to right:
brooch, $165; dress clip, $145;
and another dress clip, $95
(also has red rhinestones
and red glass cabochon).*

Clear rhinestone pieces, from top:
Coro Duette, $265, and pot metal Clipmate, $110.

Pot metal pins, from top: bar with clear rhinestones, $52;
bar with clear rhinestones, $32; and Art Deco
with clear rhinestones and green glass, $62.

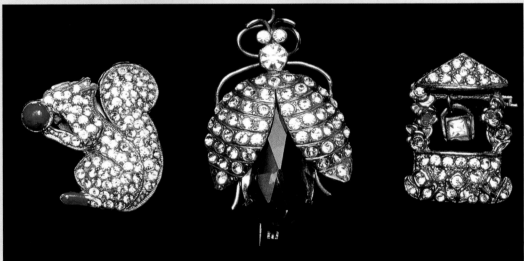

Pot metal brooches, from left: squirrel with clear rhinestones and enameling, $85;
bug with clear rhinestones and faceted glass, $145,
and wishing well with clear, red, and green rhinestones, $95.

Pot metal, from top:
heart brooch with clear
and red rhinestones, $95, and
earrings with clear rhinestones
and red cabochons, $65.

About the Author

If you have been in the world of vintage costume jewelry collecting for any time at all, you have probably seen, or at least heard about the *Hidden Treasures: Collector's Guide to Antique and Vintage Jewelry* video series. This award-winning video series was produced and co-written by Leigh Leshner and her production company, Venture Entertainment Group, Inc. The video series has won numerous awards, including Cindy Awards, The Golden Apple Award, Telly Awards, Communicator Awards, Videographer Awards, and Joey Awards.

Leigh has been collecting vintage jewelry since she was 11 and has been a dealer for more than 12 years. She participates in antiques shows, provides appraisal services, has done appraisal work for eppraisals.com, and sells her jewelry through her Web site, Thanks for the Memories at www.tias.com/stores/memories.

Leigh completed her undergraduate studies at Boston University in the College of Communication. She graduated with a bachelor of science in broadcasting and film, with a minor in marketing. She went on to continue her academic achievements at the University of California at Los Angeles, earning her master of fine arts degree in the Independent Film and Television Producers Program.

In January of 1991, Leigh created Venture Entertainment Group, Inc., a film, television, and video production company.

Bibliography

Brown, Marcia. *Unsigned Beauties of Costume Jewelry*.
   Paducah, Kentucky: Collector Books, 2000.

Brown, Marcia and Leigh Leshner. *Hidden Treasures: Rhinestone Jewelry*.
   Los Angeles, California: Venture Entertainment Group, Inc., 1998.

Dolan, Maryanne. *Collecting Rhinestone & Colored Jewelry*.
   Florence, Alabama: Books Americana, 1993.

Leshner, Leigh and Christie Romero. *Hidden Treasures: A Collector's Guide
   to Antique and Vintage Jewelry of the 19th and 20th Centuries.*
   Los Angeles, California: Venture Entertainment Group, Inc., 1992.

Matlins, Antoinette. *Jewelry & Gems: The Buying Guide*.
   Woodstock, Vermont: Gemstone Press, 1997.

Tucker, Andrew and Tamsin Kingswell. *Fashion: A Crash Course*.
   New York, New York: Watson-Guptill Publications, 2000.

Index

Art Deco, 6, 7, 18, 19, 24, 28, 33, 38, 44, 46, 47, 49, 64, 68, 83, 84, 85, 101, 119, 125, 126, 129, 131, 147, 157, 159, 164, 175, 188, 197, 205

Art Nouveau, 7

Austria, 10

baguette, 13

bangle(s), 9, 35, 37, 96, 168, 187

base metal, 6, 16, 171

bead set, 14, 15

bezel set, 14, 15

bobby pin, 72

bracelet, 19, 35, 40, 50, 52, 74, 76, 77, 78, 101, 102, 104, 123, 137, 143, 144, 154, 159, 172, 184, 186, 189, 197, 198, 199, 202, 204

bracelets, 7, 9, 18, 36, 41, 44, 45, 46, 52, 53, 59, 74, 75, 76, 78, 80, 92, 95, 97, 99, 142, 145, 191, 199

brooch(es), 7, 8, 9, 19, 21, 22, 23, 24, 25, 26, 27, 28, 29, 30, 31, 32, 33, 39, 40, 43, 48, 49, 50, 52, 53, 54, 56, 57, 58, 60, 61, 62, 63, 64, 65, 66, 67, 69, 70, 71, 72, 79, 81, 85, 100, 101, 102, 103, 104, 105, 106, 107, 108, 109, 110, 111, 112, 113, 114, 115, 116, 117, 118, 119, 120, 121, 122, 124, 125, 126, 127, 128, 129, 130, 131, 132, 133, 134, 135, 136, 137, 138, 139, 140, 141, 143, 144, 146, 147, 152, 153, 154, 155, 157, 158, 159, 160, 161, 162, 163, 164, 165, 166, 167, 169, 170, 171, 172, 173, 174, 175, 176, 177, 178, 179, 180, 181, 182, 183, 185, 186, 187, 188, 189, 190, 191, 192, 194, 197, 198, 199, 201, 202, 203, 204, 205

buckle(s), 9, 37, 45, 46, 75, 78, 112, 191

buttons, 195

cabochon(s), 26, 28, 30, 32, 33, 41, 45, 50, 53, 57, 59, 63, 67, 70, 81, 87, 90, 91, 96, 98, 100, 101, 105, 109, 111, 115, 116, 117, 118, 121, 126, 128, 130, 134, 141, 144, 145, 158, 168, 169, 171, 172, 178, 181, 191, 204, 205

channel set, 14, 15

chaton, 12

chromium, 16, 17

Clipmate, 8, 22, 182, 205

Coro, 8, 18, 22, 81, 109, 119, 127, 128, 182, 183, 186, 205

Corocraft, 18, 67, 107, 122, 139, 160, 179

Cushion cut, 12

Czechoslovakian, 10, 78

Diamond Bar, 74, 75, 78, 97

dress clip(s), 8, 9, 28, 34, 43, 49, 51, 100, 108, 113, 120, 124, 153, 154, 155, 156, 158, 161, 162, 163, 164, 168, 169, 170, 171, 174, 175, 177, 178, 179, 181, 185, 187, 189, 190, 192, 195, 197, 198, 203, 204

Duette, 7, 8, 22, 109, 119, 129, 170, 182, 205

earring(s), 7, 9, 19, 46, 47, 48, 49, 50, 52, 55, 69, 71, 73, 85, 86, 87, 88, 89, 90, 91, 92, 93, 94, 103, 104, 105, 109, 119, 122, 134, 135, 137, 138, 139, 140, 143, 144, 148, 151, 152, 156, 159, 164, 168, 172, 174, 184, 186, 189, 194, 195, 199, 202, 204, 205

Edwardian, 7

Eisenberg, 18, 24, 50, 151, 178, 179, 181, 183, 187

emerald cut, 13

filigree, 35, 37, 77, 85, 193

flat-back, 13

fur clip(s), 8, 9, 21, 29, 31, 34, 60, 71, 111, 130, 135, 158, 163, 165, 171, 175, 178, 180, 181, 183, 184, 185, 187

glass, 10, 11, 13, 38, 41, 46, 52, 55, 61, 68, 77, 82, 83, 84, 86, 87, 88, 90, 93, 94, 96, 97, 101, 102, 105, 107, 116, 123, 125, 127, 140, 143, 145, 147, 153, 156, 157, 159, 164, 168, 169, 174, 180, 183, 188, 189, 190, 191, 204, 205

hair clip, 72

hand set, 14, 15

hand set with metal prongs, 14, 15

hat pin, 9

marcasites, 38, 134, 162, 183

mine cut, 13

molded glass, 7, 13, 55, 56, 61, 81, 104, 114, 141, 143, 147, 156, 179

navette, 12

necklace(s), 9, 19, 37, 38, 40, 41, 42, 44, 54, 55, 68, 73, 80, 82, 83, 84, 86, 87, 88, 93, 94, 95, 99, 101, 104, 123, 144, 148, 149, 150, 168, 187, 188, 189, 196, 198, 199, 200

nickel silver, 16

open-back, 27, 43, 48, 60, 61, 81, 85, 94, 104, 105, 107, 111, 119, 129, 138, 140, 144, 161, 171, 172, 177, 178, 181, 183, 186, 189, 199, 201, 203, 204

Ora, 39, 69, 117

oval, 12

pave set, 14, 15

Pennino, 18, 19, 40, 42, 47, 104, 109, 116, 149

pewter, 16

pot metal, 16, 21, 22, 25, 28, 30, 32, 39, 40, 41, 43, 44, 45, 46, 47, 48, 49, 50, 51, 52, 53, 56, 57, 58, 59, 60, 61, 62, 63, 64, 65, 66, 67, 69, 70, 72, 74, 75, 76, 78, 79, 80, 81, 84, 85, 86, 87, 89, 91, 92, 94, 95, 98, 99, 100, 104, 106, 107, 108, 109, 110, 111, 112, 113, 115, 116, 117, 119, 120, 121, 122, 125, 126, 127, 128, 129, 130, 131, 132, 133, 134, 135, 136, 138, 140, 141, 142, 143, 146, 147, 151, 153, 154, 155,

156, 157, 158, 159, 161, 162, 163, 164, 165, 166, 167, 168, 169, 170, 171, 173, 174, 175, 176, 178, 179, 180, 181, 182, 183, 184, 185, 186, 189, 190, 191, 192, 194, 195, 197, 198, 202, 203, 204, 205

princess cut, 13

Reja, 18, 48, 52, 74, 85, 140, 144

rhinestone(s), 5, 7, 8, 9, 10, 11, 12, 13, 14, 19, 21, 22, 23, 24, 25, 26, 27, 28, 29, 30, 31, 32, 33, 34, 35, 36, 37, 38, 39, 40, 41, 42, 43, 44, 45, 46, 47, 48, 49, 50, 51, 52, 53, 54, 55, 56, 57, 58, 59, 60, 61, 62, 63, 64, 65, 66, 67, 68, 69, 70, 71, 72, 73, 74, 75, 76, 78, 79, 80, 81, 82, 83, 84, 85, 86, 87, 88, 89, 90, 91, 92, 93, 94, 95, 96, 97, 98, 99, 100, 101, 102, 103, 104, 105, 106, 107, 108, 109, 110, 111, 112, 113, 114, 115, 116, 117, 118, 119, 120, 121, 122, 123, 124, 125, 126, 127, 128, 129, 130, 131, 132, 133, 134, 135, 138, 139, 140, 141, 142, 143, 144, 145, 146, 147, 148, 149, 150, 151, 152, 153, 154, 155, 156, 157, 158, 159, 160, 161, 162, 163, 164, 165, 166, 167, 168, 169, 170, 171, 172, 173, 174, 175, 176, 177, 178, 179, 180, 181, 182, 183, 184, 185, 186, 187, 188, 189, 190, 191, 192, 193, 194, 195, 196, 197, 198, 199, 200, 201, 202, 203, 204, 205

rhodium, 16, 17, 21, 25, 27, 36, 37, 40, 49, 56, 58, 59, 60, 61, 63, 64, 66, 67, 69, 70, 75, 76, 78, 79, 80, 81, 91, 92, 97, 99, 100, 101, 103, 105, 108, 113, 115, 116, 119, 121, 122, 125, 126, 128, 130, 135, 137, 140, 141, 142, 143, 147, 151, 157, 159, 162, 163, 168, 171, 172, 174, 176, 178, 182, 183, 184, 187, 192, 194, 199, 201, 203

ring(s), 9, 56, 147, 168, 189, 204

rose cut, 13

scarf holder, 9, 56

sterling, 6, 16, 36, 39, 45, 50, 53, 56, 58, 59, 72, 75, 78, 84, 85, 87, 90, 92, 94, 97, 98, 101, 103, 104, 105, 107, 109, 111, 115, 117, 122, 123, 143, 145, 147, 159, 160, 164, 168, 172, 179, 181, 183, 190, 191, 192, 194, 195, 199, 204

stickpin(s), 9, 104, 133

Swarovski, 10, 11

sweetheart jewelry, 8

trembler, 8, 63, 64, 65, 103, 118, 127, 159, 185

Trifari, 8, 18, 21, 27, 31, 45, 49, 50, 60, 74, 135, 137, 145, 150, 151, 160, 171, 175, 178, 181, 182, 184, 185, 187, 194

white metal, 5, 7, 8, 16

White Period, 7